Tanks and jeeps of the U.S. Third Army roll across the Rhine on a pontoon bridge at the town of Boppard on March 27, 1945. By the end of the month seven Allied armies had crossed the mighty river, Germany's last natural barrier on the Western Front, to begin the final assault on Hitler's Third Reich.

ACROSS THE RHINE

Other Publications:
THE EPIC OF FLIGHT
THE GOOD COOK
THE SEAFARERS
THE ENCYCLOPEDIA OF COLLECTIBLES
THE GREAT CITIES
HOME REPAIR AND IMPROVEMENT
THE WORLD'S WILD PLACES
THE TIME-LIFE LIBRARY OF BOATING
HUMAN BEHAVIOR
THE ART OF SEWING
THE OLD WEST
THE EMERGENCE OF MAN
THE AMERICAN WILDERNESS
THE TIME-LIFE ENCYCLOPEDIA OF GARDENING
LIFE LIBRARY OF PHOTOGRAPHY
THIS FABULOUS CENTURY
FOODS OF THE WORLD
TIME-LIFE LIBRARY OF AMERICA
TIME-LIFE LIBRARY OF ART
GREAT AGES OF MAN
LIFE SCIENCE LIBRARY
THE LIFE HISTORY OF THE UNITED STATES
TIME READING PROGRAM
LIFE NATURE LIBRARY
LIFE WORLD LIBRARY
FAMILY LIBRARY:
    HOW THINGS WORK IN YOUR HOME
    THE TIME-LIFE BOOK OF THE FAMILY CAR
    THE TIME-LIFE FAMILY LEGAL GUIDE
    THE TIME-LIFE BOOK OF FAMILY FINANCE

Previous World War II Volumes:
Prelude to War
Blitzkrieg
The Battle of Britain
The Rising Sun
The Battle of the Atlantic
Russia Besieged
The War in the Desert
The Home Front: U.S.A.
China-Burma-India
Island Fighting
The Italian Campaign
Partisans and Guerrillas
The Second Front
Liberation
Return to the Philippines
The Air War in Europe
The Resistance
The Battle of the Bulge
The Road to Tokyo
Red Army Resurgent
The Nazis

WORLD WAR II · TIME-LIFE BOOKS · ALEXANDRIA, VIRGINIA

BY FRANKLIN M. DAVIS JR.
AND THE EDITORS OF TIME-LIFE BOOKS

ACROSS THE RHINE

Time-Life Books Inc.
is a wholly owned subsidiary of
TIME INCORPORATED

Founder: Henry R. Luce 1898-1967

Editor-in-Chief: Henry Anatole Grunwald
Chairman of the Board: Andrew Heiskell
President: James R. Shepley
Editorial Director: Ralph Graves
Vice Chairman: Arthur Temple

TIME-LIFE BOOKS INC.

Managing Editor: Jerry Korn
Executive Editor: David Maness
Assistant Managing Editors: Dale M. Brown
(planning), George Constable, George G. Daniels
(acting), Martin Mann, John Paul Porter
Art Director: Tom Suzuki
Chief of Research: David L. Harrison
Director of Photography: Robert G. Mason
Senior Text Editor: Diana Hirsh
Assistant Art Director: Arnold C. Holeywell
Assistant Chief of Research: Carolyn L. Sackett
Assistant Director of Photography: Dolores A. Littles

Chairman: Joan D. Manley
President: John D. McSweeney
Executive Vice Presidents: Carl G. Jaeger,
John Steven Maxwell, David J. Walsh
Vice Presidents: George Artandi (comptroller);
Stephen L. Bair (legal counsel); Peter G. Barnes;
Nicholas Benton (public relations); John L. Canova;
Beatrice T. Dobie (personnel); Carol Flaumenhaft
(consumer affairs); Nicholas J. C. Ingleton (Asia);
James L. Mercer (Europe/South Pacific);
Herbert Sorkin (production); Paul R. Stewart
(marketing)

WORLD WAR II

Editorial Staff for Across the Rhine
Editor: Gerald Simons
Picture Editor/Designer: Raymond Ripper
Text Editors: Bobbie Conlan, Brian McGinn,
Mark M. Steele
Staff Writers: Kathleen Burke, Peter Kaufman,
Glenn Martin McNatt, John Newton
Researchers: Charlie Clark, Betty Ajemian,
LaVerle Berry, Marion F. Briggs, Mary G. Burns,
Lucinda Moore, Cronin Buck Sleeper, Jean Strong
Art Assistant: Mary L. Orr
Editorial Assistant: Connie Strawbridge

Special Contributor
Paula York (research)

Editorial Production
Production Editor: Douglas B. Graham
Operations Manager: Gennaro C. Esposito,
Gordon E. Buck (assistant)
Assistant Production Editor: Feliciano Madrid
Quality Control: Robert L. Young (director),
James J. Cox (assistant), Daniel J. McSweeney,
Michael G. Wight (associates)
Art Coordinator: Anne B. Landry
Copy Staff: Susan B. Galloway (chief), Victoria Lee,
Barbara F. Quarmby, Celia Beattie
Picture Department: Alvin L. Ferrell

Correspondents: Elisabeth Kraemer (Bonn);
Margot Hapgood, Dorothy Bacon, Lesley Coleman
(London); Susan Jonas, Lucy T. Voulgaris (New York);
Maria Vincenza Aloisi, Josephine du Brusle (Paris);
Ann Natanson (Rome). Valuable assistance was
also provided by: Wibo van de Linde (Amsterdam);
Martha Mader (Bonn); Brian Davis, Gail Ridgewell
(London); Carolyn T. Chubet, Villette Harris,
Miriam Hsia, Christina Lieberman (New York);
John Scott (Ontario, Ottawa); Dag Christensen (Oslo);
M. T. Hirschkoff (Paris); Mimi Murphy (Rome).

The Author: FRANKLIN M. DAVIS JR., a retired major
general, is a former Commandant of the U.S. Army
War College and head of the U.S. Army Military History Institute. In World War II he served as a major
with airborne and tank troops during the crossing of
the Rhine. He is a Fellow in The Company of Military
Historians, a member of The Ends of the Earth Society
and a writer of military history and adventure fiction.

The Consultant: COLONEL JOHN R. ELTING, USA
(Ret.), is a military historian and author of The Battle
of Bunker's Hill, The Battles of Saratoga and Military
History and Atlas of the Napoleonic Wars. He edited
Military Uniforms in America: The Era of the Ameri-
can Revolution, 1755-1795 and Military Uniforms in
America: Years of Growth, 1796-1851, and was asso-
ciate editor of The West Point Atlas of American Wars.

Library of Congress Cataloguing in Publication Data

Davis, Franklin M.   1918-
   Across the Rhine.

   (World War II; v. 22)
   Bibliography: p.
   Includes index.
   1. World War, 1939-1945—Campaigns—Germany.
2. Germany—History—1933-1945.   I. Time-Life Books.
II. Title.   III. Series.
D757.D38   940.54'21   79-27301
ISBN 0-8094-2544-0
ISBN 0-8094-2543-2 lib. bdg.

For information about any Time-Life book, please write:

Reader Information
Time-Life Books
541 North Fairbanks Court
Chicago, Illinois 60611

CONTENTS

BUILD-UP FOR A NEW D-DAY

A U.S. Navy LCM landing craft, hauled overland by a tank transporter, joins the armada gathering for the Allies' assault on the Rhine in March 1945.

AN OPERATION TO RIVAL NORMANDY

In late January, 1945, even as the Allies were driving Hit
ler's armies out of Belgium in the Battle of the Bulge, Ameri
can and British support troops were hurrying along prepara
tions for the final phase of the war in Western Europe: the
crossing of the majestic Rhine River, followed by the drive
into the heartland of the Third Reich. Logistically, this oper
ation rivaled the Normandy invasion in magnitude and
complexity. Nearly four million troops, and a daily total of
at least 500 tons of supplies for each of 85 combat divisions
would have to be sent across the Rhine—presumably after
the retreating Germans had destroyed every bridge.

As the Allies fought their way toward the Rhineland,
bomb-damaged roads and railways were repaired and im
mense quantities of ammunition, gasoline and foodstuffs
were moved up from coastal ports, mostly by train and
truck. One truck line, the ABC Haul (for its American, Brit
ish and Canadian planners), pioneered an efficient relay
system to avoid traffic jams at the key port of Antwerp. Two
companies of ABC truck tractors shuttled heavily laden trail
ers to an inland marshaling point, called a surge pool, and
returned with empties. The loaded trailers were picked up a
the surge pool by the line's other truck companies, which
delivered the goods to camouflaged depots near the front
line. By this method, the ABC Haul brought up 245,000
tons of supplies in 117 days.

The most difficult task—one that taxed the ingenuity and
tempers of the Army engineers—was transporting massive
bridging materials and big landing craft such as troop
carrying LCVPs and even larger LCMs that could ferry tanks
and trucks. Great convoys of diesel truck tractors with
10-ton semitrailers had to inch through narrow, twisting vil
lage streets hauling 100-foot-long bridge pilings and LCMs
14 feet wide. The big loads went through—even if bulldoz
ers had to knock down buildings that blocked the way.

By March, American engineers alone had stockpiled in
forward depots 124 landing craft, 1,100 assault boats, and
enough lumber, pontoons and prefabricated structural sec
tions to build 62 bridges across the Rhine.

A driver on the ABC route hands over a load bill as he leaves a Belgian supply dump. Runs from Antwerp to forward depots averaged 90 miles.

Pontoons, floats and other gear to bridge the Rhine await truck transpor on the Antwerp docks, opened to Allied shipping in November 1944

A tattooed sailor and his mates camouflage LCM landing craft with olive-drab paint. Even the identifying "USN" succumbs to the brush.

A flotilla of LCMs gets a final going-over on a Belgian canal before being trucked overland to the Rhine. Aboard the landing craft in the foreground, GIs clean 20mm antiaircraft guns.

323

29729

11

Boxcars laden with Bailey-bridge girders (foreground) leave a Belgian railyard en route to a storage depot near the Rhineland.

Carrying pontoon boats and bridge-building floats, a long convoy of U.S. First Army semitrailers stops near the Rhine at Remagen.

13

BAILEY-BRIDGE PANELS

IRON ANCHORS FOR MARKER BUOYS

MARKER BUOYS

Viewed from the air, a huge depot of bridging materials extends inland from the Netherlands' Maas River in a neat grid of blocks and streets. Bridges built from the supplies in this particular dump supported the U Ninth Army's drive across the Rhine River into the industrial Ruhr.

ASSAULT BOATS

PILES OF ROPE

CONCRETE ANCHORS FOR BUOYS

Silhouetted atop a giant outboard motor, an engineer looks out over acres of bridge-building equipment in a depot near the front line. Such motors propelled ponderous barges equipped with heavy pile drivers that were used to build more or less permanent highway and railway bridges across the Rhine.

1

On the afternoon of January 24, 1945, Lieut. General Omar N. Bradley, the amiable and usually soft-spoken commander of the U.S. Twelfth Army Group in Europe, put on a display of temper that would long be remembered by those who witnessed it. The incident took place toward the end of a meeting between Bradley and his deputy commanders, Lieut. General Courtney H. Hodges and Lieut. General George S. Patton, and clouded what had otherwise been a thoroughly agreeable session.

The conferees, closeted at Patton's headquarters in Luxembourg, had every reason for good cheer when the meeting began. Thanks to the courage and tenacity of the American troops under their leadership, the unexpected German counteroffensive in the Ardennes region of Belgium had been beaten back. The way was now clear to pursue the grand Allied strategy that the Battle of the Bulge had temporarily interrupted: a massive sweep by American, British and French forces into Germany itself—through the Siegfried Line, the steel-and-concrete West Wall that the Germans had built to seal their western border, across the great natural barrier of the Rhine River and into the heart of Adolf Hitler's Third Reich.

At last the end of the War was in sight. The legions Hitler had sent forth to conquer the world were now reduced to fighting for their own homeland. Already beleaguered by the Russians on the east, they were about to encounter another juggernaut moving in from the west: an Allied war machine with a superiority over the Germans of 10 to 1 in tanks, more than 3 to 1 in planes, at least 2.5 to 1 in artillery and nearly 4 to 1 in troops. The crushing of Hitler's Reich—which the Führer had once boasted would flourish for 1,000 years—appeared to be a matter of only a few months, perhaps even weeks.

Bradley and his commanders were eager to get on with their part of the job. They were, in fact, meeting specifically to fix the boundaries between Hodges' First Army and Patton's Third as they broke through the West Wall. Agreement had been easily reached, and Hodges had declared his readiness to launch his prong of the attack on Sunday, just four days hence, when a telephone call touched off Omar Bradley's unprecedented fit of temper.

The call came from the headquarters of the Supreme Allied Commander in Europe, General Dwight D. Eisenhow-

INVADING THE THIRD REICH

er. The caller was Eisenhower's deputy chief of planning and operations, Major General John F. M. Whiteley of the British Army. Whiteley's purpose was to request—in effect, order—that Bradley turn over several of his divisions to another sector of the front facing Germany: the so-called Colmar pocket in eastern France, where a sizable number of German troops were still holding out.

Bradley was at first flabbergasted, then furious. Though the task of cleaning out the pocket belonged to American and French forces under Lieut. General Jacob L. Devers' U.S. Sixth Army Group, Bradley had already agreed to send three of his divisions to help. Now he was being asked to send more, and he hit the ceiling. Soon Whiteley turned over the phone to his American superior, Major General Harold R. Bull. But Bull had no better luck with Bradley than Whiteley had.

The men with Bradley listened in awe to the unfamiliar sound of his voice seething with anger as he argued on. Diverting additional divisions from his own impending operation to the mop-up effort, he said, would be subordinating the main event to a sideshow—putting a matter of routine tactics ahead of major strategic considerations.

Evidently sensing that he was getting nowhere with his protest, Bradley finally exploded. "If you feel that way about it," he roared into the phone, "you can take any goddam division and/or corps in the Twelfth Army Group, do with them as you see fit, and those of us that you leave back will set on our ass until hell freezes. I trust you do not think I am angry, but I want to impress upon you that I am goddam well incensed."

The outburst—later preserved on paper by Patton's chief of staff, Brigadier General Hobart R. Gay—brought a cheer of approval from Bradley's companions. As Gay recalled it: "Practically every officer in the room stood up and applauded, and General Patton said in a voice that could be heard over the telephone, 'Tell them to go to hell and all three of us will resign. I will lead the procession.' "

That night Patton's diary recorded the suspicion that the proposal to strip Bradley of some of his troops—though ostensibly intended to aid a fellow American, General Devers—was actually a devious scheme concocted by the British to ensure that the leading role in the Allied drive into Germany would go to their own top commander in Europe,

Field Marshal Sir Bernard L. Montgomery. Clearly, diverting divisions from Bradley would hamper his initial thrust into the Rhineland. "If our attacks fail after a good try," Patton sourly concluded, "we will have to give Monty troops, and the Americans simply sit on the defensive while U.S. blood aids British prestige."

Contrary to Patton's somewhat paranoid view of British intentions, the decision to reinforce the Colmar operation was, in fact, Eisenhower's; it was based on the need to eliminate a potentially troublesome German position to the rear of the Allies as they moved into Germany. Still, the American commanders could not shake the feeling that the British wielded undue influence on Eisenhower. They were pained by Ike's sunny insistence that Allied quarrels over strategy or tactics were nothing more than "family squabbles." For their part, they believed that behind the façade of Allied amity the British still viewed the Americans as the fractious colonials of 1775, who had to be kept in check lest Great Britain's own national interests suffer. As a corollary, the U.S. generals believed that the British seldom proposed any military move—however persuasive it might be to Eisenhower on its merits—if it did not somehow fit in with Britain's broad aims as a world power.

The Americans were especially wary of Montgomery—for a number of reasons. They scented an effort at self-glorification in the famous showman's flair that Montgomery's own troops loved. They were put off by what they saw as his peculiarly British talent for making people feel inferior without actually uttering an offensive word. But mostly they resented his all-knowing attitude on matters military.

Montgomery was indeed supremely self-confident—and he had every reason to be. He was more experienced at all levels of field command than any of his Allied colleagues, including Eisenhower and Bradley. He was the victor in North Africa over the great "Desert Fox," Erwin Rommel, and the Afrika Korps. Not surprisingly, he felt that he was better qualified than anyone else to guide the Allied course in the final battle for Europe.

But Montgomery had suffered some severe reverses in recent months. As the Americans viewed it, a steep price had been paid for some of Montgomery's proposals that Eisenhower had found persuasive. The Americans cited the failed British breakout at Caen in northwestern France in July of

England

North Sea

Netherlands

Rotterdam

Arnhem

Nijmegen

Emmerich

Maas River

Cleves

CANADIAN FIRST
ARMY

Kalkar   Xanten

Goch-
Udem

Geldern   Wesel

BRITISH SECOND
ARMY

Antwerp

Mörs

Krefeld

Emden

Wilhelmshaven

Hamburg

Bremen

Ems River

Lingen

Bergen-B
Ue

Stolzenau   Celle

Weser River

Dortmund-Ems
Canal

Hanover

Minden

Münster

Hameln

Bruns
Hildesheim

Lippe River

RUHR

Lippe Lateral Canal

Dortmund

Blanken
Braunla

Göttingen

Nordhaus

Kassel

Brussels

Belgium

Roermond

München Gladbach

Jüchen

U.S. NINTH
ARMY

Immendorf

Aldenhoven

Maastricht   Aachen

Namur

Oberkassel
Düsseldorf
Neuss

Roer River

Erft River

Jülich

Schmidt

Monschau

U.S. FIRST
ARMY

Gemünd

France

Meuse River

A
R
D
E
N
N
E
S

Cologne

Bonn
Düren

Ruhr River

Remagen

Ahr River

Buchenw

Eisenach
Gotha
Ohrdruf

Merkers

Germany

Prüm

Kyll River

EIFEL

Coblenz

Rhine River

U.S.
THIRD
ARMY

Luxembourg

Bitburg

P
A
L
A
T
I
N
A
T
E

Wiesbaden   Frankfurt

Hammelburg

Kronac

Rheims

Quierschied
Herrensohr

Oppenheim   Aschaffenburg

Lohr

Schweinfurt

Bamberg

Versailles

Sulzbach
Dudweiler

S
A
A
R

Oppenheim

Würzburg

Bayre

U.S.
SEVENTH
ARMY

Bad Dürkheim

Saar River

Nuremberg

Heilbronn   Geisselhardt

FRENCH
FIRST
ARMY

Scheibenhardt
Karlsruhe

B
L
A
C
K

F
O
R
E
S
T

Stuttgart

Ellingen

Seine River

Moselle River

Berneck

Neckar River

Danube River

Colmar

Rhine River

Lower Rhine River

Dachau
Mun

WEST WALL

ALLIED TERRITORY
FEBRUARY 1945

Switzerland

0   20   40   60   80   100

Scale of Miles

20

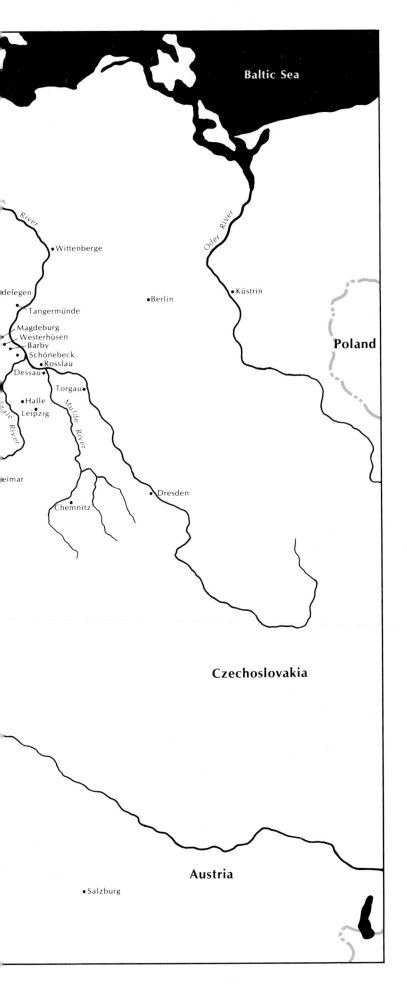

Baltic Sea

River

• Wittenberge

Oder River

delegen

• Berlin

• Küstrin

Poland

Tangermünde

Magdeburg
Westerhüsen
Barby
Schönebeck
• Rosslau

Dessau

Torgau

• Halle
Leipzig

Mulde River

ale River

eimar

• Dresden

Chemnitz

Czechoslovakia

Austria

• Salzburg

By February 1945 the Allies (shaded area) were prepared to resume their eastward drive, which had been rocked backward in December by the surprise German counteroffensive in the Ardennes. All territory lost had now been recaptured, and seven Allied armies stood astride 400 miles of German border facing the West Wall defense system and the Rhine River, which were defended by seven German armies.

1944—which had cost more than 6,000 British and Canadian lives and a third of all British tanks on the Continent. The Americans cited as well the disastrous airborne Operation *Market-Garden* in Holland in September of 1944—which had cost 17,000 British, Canadian and American dead, wounded or captured.

As overall commander of both operations, Montgomery had come in for heavy criticism from his American colleagues. The simmering American irritation with Montgomery had then boiled up in open anger in early January, 1945, when—at a well-publicized press conference—the flamboyant field marshal all but claimed primary credit for the successful outcome of the Battle of the Bulge. The British press naturally trumpeted that good old "Monty" had been the savior of the beleaguered Yanks. As General Bradley bitterly put it, Montgomery was pictured "as having single-handedly rescued our shattered American armies."

British Prime Minister Winston S. Churchill himself had quickly moved to mollify the outraged Americans. In a speech given before the House of Commons, he had proclaimed the battle a decidedly American victory, pointing out that U.S. troops had outnumbered the British by 30 or 40 to 1 and that the Americans had lost 60 or 80 men to every British soldier lost.

But Churchill's effort to undo Montgomery's blunder had not sufficed. Bradley and his commanders remained convinced that the field marshal was up to even more serious business than his press-conference performance—and they were quite right. Montgomery was still fervently seeking, after several futile tries, to persuade Eisenhower to give him full command of the Allied drive into Germany.

A few days after the telephone incident at Patton's headquarters, Bradley appeared at Eisenhower's office in Versailles for some blunt talk about Montgomery. Bradley, a small-town boy from Missouri, and Eisenhower, a small-town boy from Kansas, spoke the same down-to-earth language. Moreover, they were old friends—both graduates of the West Point class of 1915.

Bradley tersely summed up his view of the situation. He had been assured at the highest level of U.S. military authority—by Army Chief of Staff George C. Marshall—that he would never be "sandwiched" under British command. Yet it now appeared that Montgomery, abetted by a snowballing campaign in the British press, was about to be handed control of all Allied ground forces. If that were to happen, Bradley told Eisenhower, "you must send me home, for if Montgomery goes in over me, I will have lost the confidence of my command."

Years later, Bradley still vividly remembered the exchange that followed:

"Ike flushed. He stiffened in his chair and eyed me hotly. 'Well—' he said, 'I thought you were the one person I could count on for doing anything I asked you to.'

" 'You can, Ike,' I said. 'I've enjoyed every bit of my service with you. But this is one thing I cannot take.' "

There the matter rested. Bradley went back to his tactical headquarters at Namur in Belgium. Eisenhower went back to sorting out the complexities of the coming assault on the German homeland. Among his problems, he confessed in a private message to General Marshall, was the wearisome task of "trying to arrange the blankets smoothly over several prima donnas in the same bed."

Eisenhower's skill at reconciling differences within the Allied camp was facing its greatest test. The British-American teamwork that he had so carefully nurtured, from the plan-ning of the North African invasion in 1942 to the execution of the Normandy landings two years later, was critical for the advance into Germany. Yet the team was now threatening to come apart.

More than a clash of personalities was involved. However much Montgomery grated on Bradley and his associates, surface relations were correct and sometimes even cordial. The chief problem stemmed from a sharp divergence of views on the strategy to be employed in piercing Germany's western defenses.

The British favored a powerful single thrust under Montgomery's command, using most of the available fighting men to slash into northwestern Germany and cross a 20-mile section of the Rhine River north of the Ruhr district. Beyond the Rhine at this point lay the level terrain of the north German plain, which would offer, Montgomery said, relatively easy access to the interior of the Reich. The Americans, on the other hand, favored a broad-front strategy, by which their armies would move into Germany all along the western border and cross the Rhine at several widely separated places, providing a choice of directions for the follow-through strike.

To the British, the broad-front plan smacked of a slap-

dash, attack-everywhere-at-once approach summed up by one anonymous wag as "have a go, Joe"—the usual salutation by London prostitutes to passing Yanks. The Americans, for their part, viewed the single-thrust plan as an attempt by Montgomery to hog the main show while the American role was downgraded. One of the British plan's provisions specified that those U.S. troops not allotted to Montgomery's purposes were to remain in positions of static defense—in short, sidelined.

Although it was left unsaid, both strategy proposals owed a great deal to the fact that the war was winding down. By heading across the north German plain, Montgomery's forces would be able to reach such key German ports as Bremen and Hamburg before the Russians did. The Red Army was by this time only about 40 miles east of Berlin, building a bridgehead across the Oder River to the north of Küstrin and regrouping for major offensives westward. Prime Minister Churchill had no intention of letting his wartime ally of convenience, Soviet dictator Josef Stalin, embark upon the postwar era with a foothold on the North Sea, Britain's centuries-long preserve.

The motivation behind the Americans' plan was less subtle. It simply reflected their impatience. By attacking Germany on a broad front, they hoped to speed the end of the war in Europe, then turn to wrapping up the war in the Pacific, and go home at last.

Eisenhower's solution to the strategy dispute was characteristic: He gave each contending party some, but not all, of what each sought. Montgomery won top priority for his thrust in the north, but lost the attempt to take overall command and to impose a static defense on U.S. forces not involved in his operation. Instead, these forces were to go on the "aggressive defensive." Wrote Eisenhower in a letter to Montgomery: "The more Germans we kill west of the Rhine the fewer there will be to meet us east of the river."

For Bradley, the bad news from the Supreme Allied Commander was that he would have to furnish three or four divisions to support Montgomery's southern flank. On the other hand, the "aggressive defense" approved for Bradley's other forces could equally be read as authorizing a "limited offense"; in any case, it signaled that the broad-front strategy was far from dead. Moreover, Bradley was now freed of the fear that Montgomery would become his boss.

On February 2, at a meeting on the Mediterranean island of Malta, the Combined Chiefs of Staff of the United States and Great Britain approved the specifics of Eisenhower's

Britain's Field Marshal Sir Bernard L. Montgomery (left) and Lieut. General William H. Simpson, commander of the U.S. Ninth Army, survey the massive concrete dragon's-teeth tank obstacles of the West Wall, Germany's primary defense barrier west of the Rhine. The once-formidable fortifications, also known as the Siegfried Line, had fallen into disrepair during Germany's years of victory, and though Hitler rushed in 200,000 workers to refurbish the emplacements, the Allies managed to outflank and punch through them, albeit with considerable difficulty.

Back from a 36-hour trip between Cherbourg and Belgium, the brakeman of the U.S. Army's "Toot-Sweet Express" chalks an X on the engine cab to mark the crew's 13th run from the Channel to advance supply depots. In January and February of 1945, during the build-up to cross the Rhine, trains operated by the Transportation Corps delivered an average of 385 tons of supplies daily to the front.

plan for the first phase of the battle for Germany—a drive to the west bank of the Rhine. To get there from Germany's western border would require moving through an area of roughly 14,000 square miles defended by several hundred thousand German troops who were under orders from Hitler to hold at all costs. With their defeat, the west bank of the Rhine would be secured and the stage would be set for the battle's second and third phases—crossing the river to the east bank and encircling Germany's most important industrial area, the Ruhr.

The initial phase was to be put into action within a week of the Combined Chiefs' go-ahead. Montgomery's Twenty-first Army Group, at the northern end of the front facing Germany, would jump off first. The attack would commence on February 8. In an operation code-named *Veritable,* two of Montgomery's armies—the Canadian First and the British Second—were to drive southeastward from the Nijmegen area of Holland into the Rhine lowlands. Two days later, in an operation code-named *Grenade,* the U.S. Ninth Army, under the command of Lieut. General William H. Simpson, was to thrust northeastward from the Maastricht area of Holland to link up with the Canadians. The Ninth had been under Montgomery's Twenty-first Army Group since the Battle of the Bulge in December. He now meant to use it as a southern pincers, thus trapping the German forces facing the British in the center of the attack line.

To effect the linkup, the Ninth Army would have to cross the Roer River, which bisected the Dutch-German border. Although scarcely in the same class as the mighty Rhine, the Roer presented a potentially major hazard. The river and its tributaries were spanned by no fewer than seven dams, which had been built to control the flow of floodwaters into the lowlands to the north. If the Germans in control of the dams flooded the lowlands, they would not only halt the Ninth Army at the river's edge, but would also threaten the Canadians and the British in the lowlands with a washout. The task of seizing the dams to prevent this possibility was assigned to Bradley, using First Army forces under General Hodges. In further support of Montgomery's drive, elements of Hodges' army were then to cross the Roer in concert with Simpson's Ninth Army, covering Operation *Grenade's* southern flank.

General Bradley's zone—the center of the front facing Germany—was to remain relatively quiet till Montgomery reached the Rhine. Only then was Bradley to go on the offensive, pushing forward to the Rhine through the wooded highlands of the region known as the Eifel. The operation, code-named *Lumberjack,* was to begin on February 23.

At the southern end of the front, General Devers was to remain on the defensive until Bradley was at the Rhine. Then, according to the staggered plan of attack, he was to close to the river opposite his sector by sending his U.S. Seventh Army across the heavily industrialized Saar basin and the rest of the sprawling region of the Palatinate. This operation, code-named *Undertone,* was to get under way on the 15th of March.

Adolf Hitler, who had once plotted his campaigns with clockwork precision, had now totally lost the initiative. His armies were on the defensive everywhere, and he could only react to the attacks of his enemies closing in from the east and the west. Reich Marshal Hermann Göring was later to tell Allied interrogators that Hitler's tactics in early 1945 were based on "the same principle as a fire department." As between an area where flames were already crackling and an area where they were expected to break out but had not yet done so, Göring explained, "the troops were sent wherever there was a fire."

Accordingly, on January 22, with 150 to 160 Russian divisions driving toward Germany's eastern border and with its western border still relatively quiet, Hitler had ordered the transfer of major forces to confront the Red Army in the east. Of 12 panzer divisions in the west, seven were sent east, including some of the finest troops in the failed Ardennes counteroffensive—the remnants of SS General Josef "Sepp" Dietrich's Sixth Panzer Army. Moreover, the Führer decreed that virtually all of the new tanks that Germany was producing, as well as those in the repair depots, were to be sent to the Russian front. Other heavy armor was to be similarly disposed. For the month of February, the Eastern Front was allotted a total of 1,675 tanks and assault guns, the Western Front only 67.

By this time, Hitler had all but abandoned the notion that the closer the Russians got to Berlin, the more amenable the British and the Americans would be to making a separate peace with Germany. But in facing up to the reality of

Camouflage-helmeted recruits of the Volksgrenadier, or people's infantry, divisions march in formation while other conscripts practice machine gunnery at a training area in Germany in early 1945. So desperate was the Wehrmacht's need for combat-troop reinforcements that these soldiers—the very young, the overage and the previously deferred—were frequently sent into battle with only six weeks' training.

a continuance of the war in the west, the German leader made another fateful miscalculation. He estimated that in the wake of the fierce fighting in the Ardennes, the Anglo-American forces would need at least two months to regroup for their assault on Germany. In fact, Eisenhower's green light from the Combined Chiefs of Staff came on February 2, just five days after the Battle of the Bulge had been officially declared over.

With the transfers to the Eastern Front, Hitler had retained only about one million men to pit against the 3,725,000 Allied troops that Eisenhower could muster along Germany's western border. In five years of waging war in Europe, Russia and North Africa, the Wehrmacht had suffered nearly four million casualties. The Führer was now nearing the end of his manpower resources. In mid-January, he had decreed that all men under 45 who were still working in industry were to be drafted into the armed forces, and he had programed eight new divisions to be made up of youths just turned 17.

These fresh conscripts—as well as the men in the *Volks-grenadier* (people's infantry) divisions that had been put together in the latter half of 1944 from such varied sources as rear-area echelons and hastily assembled airmen and sailors—lacked the training of their seasoned comrades. But they were no more likely to flout the dictates of an authoritarian regime or the stern discipline imposed by German military tradition. Whether latecomer or veteran, the German soldier tended to keep fighting even when a situation was clearly hopeless. Those men who questioned the claim of Nazi invincibility did well to keep their doubts to themselves; as unit officers regularly reminded their troops, anyone who succumbed to "defeatist talk" ran the risk of being summarily shot.

To bolster his forces, Hitler counted on the formidable barriers to invasion from the west posed successively by the West Wall and the Rhine River. The West Wall, begun in 1936 and later extended to stretch 400 miles from Germany's border with Switzerland in the south to the Dutch frontier in the north, represented a monumental feat of construction. The fortifications were from three to more than 20

RESCUE ON A FLOODED FRONT

Marooned Canadian infantrymen, trying
to navigate an improvised raft, pole toward a
relief crew arriving by amphibious vehicle.

A convoy of amphibious rescue vehicles enters
a flooded Dutch village cheered on by
troops leaning out of a second-story window.

For the Canadian troops who started out across the Waal River on the 8th of February, 1945, the new offensive launched by Field Marshal Montgomery was marked by misery from the start. The men spent the first day of Operation *Veritable* trekking across swampy flats; everyone was mud-caked and soaked to the bone by an incessant drizzle. And by the end of the second day, hundreds of men were stranded by swiftly rising floodwaters.

The flooding was the work of retreating Germans who had dynamited the dikes as they withdrew. Within a few hours, the water had risen six feet, inundating a vast area and marooning the troops on whatever high ground they could find along the Dutch-German border.

On the night of February 9, cold, hungry soldiers roosted wherever they were trapped. Some huddled together on the decks of their stalled tanks. Others settled in the upper stories of cottages and on the roofs of barns, sharing their quarters with menageries of livestock. A few groups of infantrymen discovered less amenable neighbors—German snipers stranded on segments of dikes within firing distance.

By the following morning, however, the Canadian First Army had commenced operations to retrieve its stranded troops. The rescue teams had little trouble negotiating the floodwaters in amphibious vehicles known as buffaloes and weasels. But their maps were almost completely useless in the watery expanse, and they had to navigate by taking bearings on church steeples. Still, the convoys pushed ahead, concealed from the isolated German troops by a thick smoke screen.

The rescue operation proceeded steadily. Within 24 hours, most of the marooned soldiers had been ferried back to more or less dry land, where they were served hot meals and issued dry blankets. Soon—much sooner than the Germans had expected—the Canadians were slogging on to breach the West Wall defenses.

miles deep, depending on the terrain. Overall, the system included more than 3,000 pillboxes and blockhouses with interlocking fields of fire, supplemented by row upon row of so-called dragon's teeth—concrete pyramids, from two to five feet high, designed to stop enemy tanks. These fixed emplacements were augmented by minefields, and in recent weeks by newly dug fieldworks.

Though the Germans had neglected the maintenance of the West Wall since their victorious sweep into the Low Countries and France in 1940—and were now hastily attempting to refurbish it—the line still represented a formidable obstacle for attackers. Manned by tenacious troops, it could delay the enemy long enough to permit a counterpunch by mobile reserves. In October of 1944, the Allies had managed to breach a 40-mile segment of the wall in the vicinity of Aachen, near the Belgian border, and had succeeded in clinging to their gains despite the Ardennes counteroffensive. But the rest of the West Wall remained in German hands.

Behind the wall, 20 to 90 miles deeper into Germany, lay the Rhine River, a great natural moat against attack. From its Alpine sources in Switzerland, the river flowed 450 miles through Germany before joining the Old Maas River at Rotterdam and emptying into the North Sea. At some points, particularly along its more northerly reaches, the river was nearly half a mile wide, with swift and treacherous currents that could make navigation difficult even for heavy barges.

The Rhine's importance to the Germans went far beyond its potential role in defense of the Reich. The majestic waterway was an integral part of their national mystique, intimately bound up with their history, culture and legends. It was the setting for the opening opera of Richard Wagner's monumental tetralogy, *Ring of the Nibelung,* in which Rhine maidens held control of a ring made of Rhine gold that conferred limitless power upon its wearer. For long years the Rhine had also served as a major artery of commerce, helping build Germany's economic strength by carrying the products of industry to North Sea ports for transshipment to the world beyond.

By early 1945, most of the once-flourishing cities along the banks of the Rhine lay in ruins, grim testimony to the savage Allied aerial assault on Germany. But the river itself had taken on ever greater importance as a supply route for the German military. In accord with recent Allied air strategy, Germany's rail transport system had come under concentrated attack by U.S. and British bombers. Railways, bridges, freight yards and repair shops were in shambles. The Rhine was now the only alternative route of supply for the troops defending Germany in the west.

For Eisenhower and his commanders, the need to take the

On guard in a strange battlefield, a GI keeps German miners at work in a coal mine at Alsdorf, west of the Ruhr. German troops were still in control of other parts of the mine, and the mine shaft was rocked continuously by shells bursting on German positions overhead.

Operation Veritable, the British and Canadian drive from Nijmegen southeastward to the Rhine, called for the XXX Corps to capture Cleves and Goch, two fortified towns beyond the Reichswald, a German state forest. Since outflanking was impossible— much of the area to the north and south was flooded—the XXX Corps was to make a frontal assault directly through the forest where the German 84th Division lay in wait.

Rhine was just as urgent as Hitler's need to hang on to it. Until the river was firmly in Allied hands, the way into the rest of Germany would be effectively blocked.

Eisenhower's timetable for the drive to the Rhine required revision almost as soon as the campaign began. Operation *Veritable,* the British and Canadian move from Holland into northwest Germany, jumped off as scheduled on February

8. But Operation *Grenade,* which was designed to serve as *Veritable's* southern flank, could not make its assigned starting date of February 10; it had to be delayed for nearly two weeks. The reason was complicated.

While the responsibility for Operation *Grenade* rested with the one American army under Montgomery's command—the U.S. Ninth—the responsibility for speeding the Ninth's way into Germany rested with one of the American

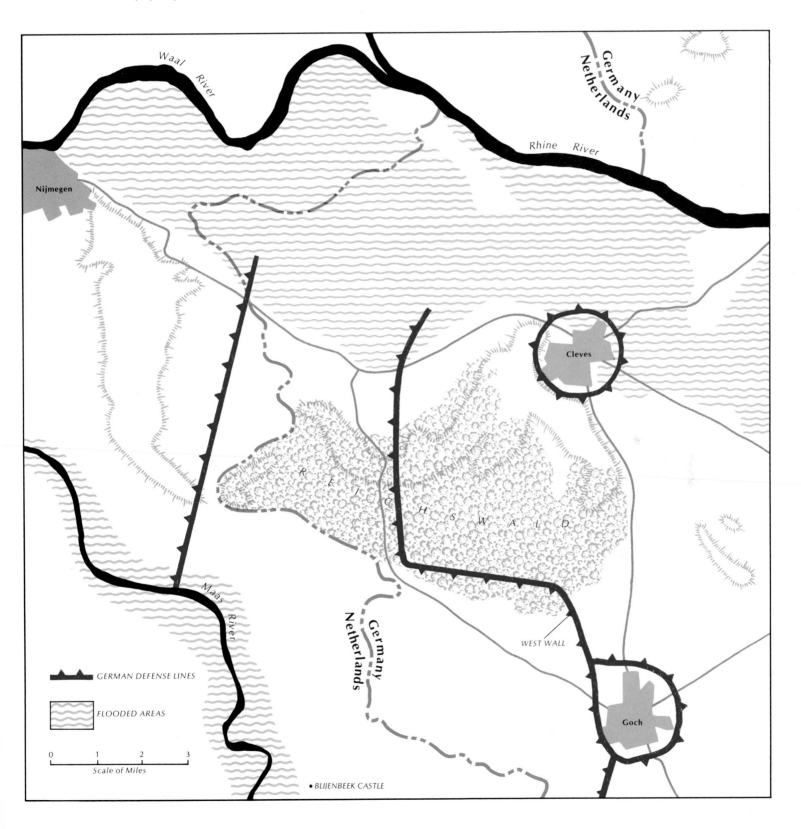

GERMAN DEFENSE LINES

FLOODED AREAS

0   1   2   3
Scale of Miles

armies under Bradley's command: the U.S. First. The First had to race to the Roer River, the Ninth's access to Germany, in time to prevent the Germans from blowing the complex of dams and turning the Roer and its tributaries into impassable torrents. Above all, the biggest of the seven dams, the Schwammenauel, had to be saved from destruction; it impounded an enormous lake five miles long and a half mile wide in places. Its loss would result in catastrophic flooding, and render meaningless the securing of the six smaller dams.

Bradley ordered an all-out dash to the Roer. The First Army's 78th Division, assigned the task of capturing the Schwammenauel, jumped off on February 5, three days before the start of *Veritable* and five days before the scheduled start of *Grenade*. The time allotted to secure the objective seemed ample, and the distance manageable. Although the terrain to be traversed was known to be difficult—its hills and ravines and thick woods had been the scene of sharp fighting prior to the Battle of the Bulge—the dam lay only about five miles northeast of the attackers' starting point near the town of Monschau, just inside the German border with Belgium.

At first, things went well for the men of the 78th. In the rainy, predawn darkness, the advance units quietly made their way past numerous enemy pillboxes and bunkers; as one checkpoint after another was reached, word went back to divisional headquarters: "No enemy contact." Then, shortly after daylight, trouble loomed. The men began to encounter small-arms fire; worse, the main highway and feeder road they were using proved to be heavily mined and cratered. The infantry had to leave behind the supporting weaponry and proceed cross-country.

As the men clambered up and down steep slopes and through dense, dimly lit patches of woods, enemy artillery and mortar fire zeroed in on them. One company was ambushed; a rumor circulated that the company had been cut to pieces. The rumor was later proved false, but the confused and jittery attackers pulled back for the night, not far from their starting point.

The German defenders of the Schwammenauel Dam were the 6,000 men of the 272nd Volksgrenadier Division—a supposedly inferior division, but manifestly well led and well deployed. On the morning of February 6, the American attack resumed. It got as far as the road leading into the town of Schmidt, which commanded the approach to the dam, but it was then stopped cold. The 272nd Volks-

grenadiers beat back several battalion-sized attempts to clear the road. Manning carefully prepared defenses, the Germans seemed invulnerable to everything the 78th Infantry could throw against them. February 6 passed, as did the 7th and the 8th. Still the Volksgrenadiers held out.

At his command post the First Army's commander, General Hodges, was painfully aware that the Ninth Army was supposed to jump off across the lower reaches of the Roer on the morning of the 10th. He rushed a regimental combat team of his 9th Division into the fight in support of the 78th. That seemed to tip the balance. Yet it was not until midnight on February 9 that the combined forces of the two U.S. divisions managed to battle their way through the Volksgrenadiers and reach the dam.

It was too late. As combat engineers of the 78th, dodging sniper fire, went racing across the top of the dam, they found that part of the spillway had been blown by German demolition teams. Frantically, the engineers slid down the 200-foot sloping face of the dam to an access tunnel, hoping to find and remove additional explosives before they could be touched off. They found no explosives, but they discovered that the Germans had destroyed the power-room machinery and the discharge valves, making it impossible to halt the flow of water.

The reservoir had a capacity of nearly 111 million cubic yards; as the contents gushed out, the breach in the Schwammenauel's spillway widened. In a few hours the level of the Roer rose five feet. From a placid stream less than 90 feet from shore to shore, the river turned into a churning lake more than a mile wide in places. The engineers estimated that it would take at least 14 days for the floodwaters to recede enough to make a crossing possible.

Operation *Grenade* would have to wait. And Operation *Veritable,* now under way, would be adversely affected. Without *Grenade* to pin down German mobile reserves, the enemy forces facing *Veritable* could be strengthened. Moreover, Montgomery's Canadian First and British Second Armies had little room to maneuver. On their left flank, the Nijmegen area had long been underwater; the Germans had breached the Dutch dikes there three months earlier. With the unleashing of the Schwammenauel Dam, the area on the right flank was now similarly inundated. The result was to limit the direction of the *Veritable* attack to the high ground directly ahead of it.

And directly ahead lay a German state forest, the Reichswald, 32 square miles of dense evergreens where visibility was often no more than a few yards. Within the Reichswald were the fortifications of the northern extension of the West Wall. Beyond the forest, the approach to the Rhine was studded with dugouts, pillboxes, minefields and antitank ditches. The towns in the area were likewise fortified, and they were defended by antiaircraft batteries, heavy mortars and mobile field guns.

Guarding the Reichswald proper were three regiments of the German 84th Division—10,000 soldiers in all—backed up by a regiment of 2,000 to 3,000 paratroopers deployed south of the forest. These were men of the First Parachute Army, under the command of Lieut. General Alfred Schlemm, a tough, shrewd veteran of the fighting on the Eastern Front. Most of Schlemm's soldiers were fresh; even more important, they were fighting on—and for—their own soil.

The weather, moreover, was on the Germans' side: Nine days before the battle got under way, an unseasonable thaw had transformed the ground of the Reichswald, difficult at best, into a swamp.

The main thrust of the *Veritable* attack had been assigned to a British force—the XXX Corps—operating under the Canadian First Army. The corps commander, Lieut. General Sir Brian G. Horrocks, was both hero and legend to his men. He had proved to be Montgomery's most brilliant deputy during the fighting in North Africa; although a bullet from a strafing Luftwaffe fighter plane had pierced his lungs and stomach and put him into the hospital for 14 months, he had scoffed at doctors' warnings that he should never again hold a field command.

Now the irrepressible Horrocks was back in action, and counting on a quick breakthrough before German reinforcements could be brought up. He believed that he had more than enough manpower: one armored and six infantry divisions, plus three armored brigades and 11 tank regiments with specialized equipment for breaching fortifications. In tanks alone, he had overwhelming superiority—500 at the front and an additional 500 in reserve, compared with barely 50 that the Germans could muster from the remnants of

The Roer River valley lies awash in floodwaters after retreating German troops destroyed the discharge valves of the huge Schwammenauel Dam on February 9, 1945. The river was impassable for two weeks, with rampaging currents that at one point reached speeds of 10 miles per hour.

two panzer divisions mauled during the Ardennes fighting.

Operation *Veritable* was preceded not only by aerial bombardment on critical links to the battle area—railways, ferries, bridges—but also by the heaviest artillery barrage of the entire war in the west. At 5 a.m. on February 8, five and a half hours before the attackers jumped off, 1,050 field guns commenced pouring half a million shells into the German positions. At the hour of departure, Horrocks' XXX Corps began working southeast along a narrow neck of land, no more than six miles wide, between flooded valleys to the left and the right. At first, there was little or no enemy fire. The troops concluded that few defenders could have survived such a bombardment. The operation looked like a walkover, and spirits were high. The occupants of one armored personnel carrier sported special headgear they had managed to scrounge—black top hats of the kind the Germans reserved for funerals.

But the joking soon ended. At daybreak a heavy rain started to fall. It was to continue virtually without letup for five days, grounding Allied air support and making the already-swampy forest floor almost impassable. From his command post—a wooden platform his engineers had built for him partway up a large tree—General Horrocks watched his unhappy troops slog forward. Among them were some of the British Empire's oldest and finest regiments, their names like a drum roll down the years: the Coldstream Guards, the Argyll and Sutherland Highlanders, the Black Watch, the Duke of Cornwall's Light Infantry, the Royal Canadian Hussars, the Fife and Forfar Yeomanry, the Queen's Own Rifles of Canada.

On the night of the 9th, Horrocks received word of what seemed like a fantastic bit of luck. Elements of his 15th Scottish Division, moving along a road on the Reichswald's northern fringes, had made their way past the forest and were approaching Cleves. This ancient town—birthplace of Henry VIII's fourth wife, Anne of Cleves—was a key objective of Operation *Veritable*. The road that led there continued on to the west bank of the Rhine.

Hoping to gain momentum, Horrocks immediately dispatched two mobile columns of his 43rd Division to pass through the 15th Scottish in Cleves and seize another key town, Goch, the anchor of the German defense line seven miles southeast of Cleves.

But the report to Horrocks was premature; the 15th Scottish was unable to enter Cleves. Its streets were pocked with craters and piled high with rubble—the result of a previous visit by Royal Air Force raiders in which they had unaccountably used high-explosive bombs instead of the incendiaries Horrocks had specified. The tanks and other vehicles of the 15th Scottish were caught in a massive jam on the road into town, with no detours possible; the fields on either side of the road were virtual lakes. As the mobile columns of the 43rd Division tried to get through in the darkness and rain, units of the two divisions became hopelessly snarled.

The Germans saw their opportunity and made the most of it. In the 36 hours or so before the attackers cleared the way into Cleves, the First Parachute Army's General Schlemm brought up two armored divisions and two paratroop divisions—reinforcements both for the town garrison and for the Reichswald defenders, large numbers of whom had survived the opening bombardment by taking refuge in underground dugouts.

The 15th Scottish had to fight for Cleves house by house. It took two days to capture the town, and by then formidable German forces awaited the XXX Corps on the road to the Rhine. Advancing inside the Reichswald was a grueling yard-by-yard process for the British and Canadians; at times, the men were wading waist-deep in icy water. The flooding, and the dense growth of the trees, confined tanks and half-tracks to the few roads and trails on high ground. And these were under constant sniper and antitank fire. It took the better part of two weeks for Horrocks' troops to bull their way through General Schlemm's 84th Division and his supporting paratroopers.

In the more open country south of the forest, Schlemm's defenders were just as full of fight. Driving eastward, the British 52nd Lowland Division was held up by heavy fire coming from Blijenbeek Castle, a medieval fortress surrounded by a water-filled moat 20 feet wide. Three separate assaults on this stronghold were repelled; one company trying to breach the walls was cut down almost to a man. Blijenbeek fell only after RAF planes had dropped nine 1,000-pound bombs on it. And then the British made a discomfiting discovery: The castle's defenders numbered just 15 paratroopers. They had been kept supplied by rafts sent across the flooded approaches by night, and their fierce determination to hold out was reflected in a sign on one of the castle's interior walls. It read: *"Sieg oder Sibirien"* ("Victory or Siberia").

On February 21, six miles northeast of Blijenbeek Castle, a more useful bastion fell: the town of Goch. The Germans had counted on Goch as a pivotal part of their defense line beyond the Reichswald. They had turned the section of the line from Cleves to Goch into one long belt of trenches, antitank ditches, minefields and barbed-wire entanglements. Villages and isolated farmhouses along the way had been transformed into fortified strong points, and Goch it-self—population 10,000—had been ringed by fieldworks.

But as three of Horrocks' divisions converged for the final attack early on February 19, the town's garrison commander surrendered. Although the British had seized most of the town, some of his men fought on—with such ferocity that two more days of street battling were required before Goch was cleared of its last defenders.

Goch was a particular prize. Its capture meant that Operation *Veritable* had expanded the constricted, six-mile-wide front from which it had started into a 20-mile front facing much easier terrain.

On February 23, Horrocks sent his troops a message of congratulations and personal thanks. About 12,000 Germans had been taken prisoner and "large numbers" (later estimated at about 8,000) killed. "You have broken through the Siegfried Line," Horrocks said, "and drawn on to yourselves the bulk of the German reserves in the west." With this first task out of the way, Horrocks informed his men, the prospect ahead was bright: "If we continue our efforts for a few more days, the German front is bound to crack." The cost to the British had been 6,000 casualties.

Almost in passing, the message from Horrocks contained a nugget of hard news more welcome to his weary troops than gentlemanly expressions of gratitude. Support from the stalled Operation *Grenade* was coming at long last: At 3:30 that morning, the U.S. Ninth Army had begun crossing the Roer River.

Two weeks after the Germans had flooded the Roer, the river was still dangerously swollen. Rain and the runoff of melting snows had helped keep the water level high and the current swift. From the Ninth Army's positions west of the river, engineers had gone out daily—sometimes creeping forward under enemy fire—to take their readings of water conditions. On February 17, with their calculations buttressed by aerial photographs of the reservoirs, the engineers had produced a long-range forecast: By about noon on the 24th, the river would drop to safe levels—and even earlier, by midnight on the 22nd, the water would have receded enough to make a crossing possible, though hazardous in the extreme.

To General Simpson, the Ninth's commander, the choice was clear. However risky, a crossing by dark—during the

An elaborate network of trenches (far left) marks the German defenses before the strategic village of Cleves near the border between Holland and Germany. So tenacious were the defenders, some of whom are shown at near left, that it took British troops equipped with flamethrowers to dislodge them and push on into the heart of Germany.

early morning hours of the 23rd—would not only hold an element of surprise but would gain more than a day's precious time; across the river, there were signs of a German build-up in the making. Furthermore, the enforced wait had begun to wear on Simpson's forces. Except for rehearsals of the crossing on some of the Roer's tributary streams, there had been little for the men to do. Some had whiled away the time enjoying the springlike warmth, playing catch with baseballs that had materialized out of nowhere. But their bivouacs, mostly damp cellars strewn with laundry and clouded with coal smoke from leaky stovepipes, were beginning to pall.

Simpson, a tall, lanky Texan who hid the fact that he suffered from serious stomach trouble, had made good use of the waiting period. Eisenhower was later to say of him that "if Simpson ever made a mistake as an Army commander, it never came to my attention." The preparations for the Roer crossing bore the stamp of faultless planning.

Simpson proposed to send six divisions across the river simultaneously, along a 17-mile stretch of the Roer marked by the towns of Linnich in the north and Düren on the opposite shore in the south. The crossing at the northern end would be made by four divisions of Simpson's Ninth Army, at the southern end by two divisions of General Hodges' First Army. Advance patrols and leading waves of infantry were to cross the river in eight-man assault boats; follow-up troops were to go over on footbridges that engineers would begin installing exactly at H-hour. At least three vehicular bridges would also be erected in each division sector.

There was to be no preliminary pounding of the target area by Allied aircraft—standard practice in other operations. Simpson did not intend to give away his show any sooner than he had to. Instead, he scheduled an opening artillery barrage to last for barely 45 minutes before his men jumped off at 3:30 a.m. But this was to be a monster barrage, fired by more than 2,000 guns—one for every 10 yards of the front.

Simpson's arsenal was filled to overflowing. A total of 46,000 tons of ammunition had been accumulated, four times the amount normally stocked by a field army. The new M24 light tank, mounting a 75mm gun, had been distributed to some of the armored divisions. There was no danger of running out of fuel; the depots held some three million gallons of gasoline.

In the week preceding the attack, more than 6,000 boxcars, rolling up to the Ninth Army front on newly repaired rail lines, brought in 45,000 tons of general supplies, including communications equipment; signal units were able to establish additional radio circuits in the Linnich area to tie all artillery and armored units together in preparation for the opening bombardment. But Simpson, determined not to alert German monitors that anything was afoot, ordered that the message traffic at command levels be held to normal and that total radio silence be enforced between tactical units. Simpson's insistence on absolute security was all-encompassing. To prevent the Germans from guessing the strength and identity of the Ninth Army's dispositions, he ordered the removal of vehicle markings and uniform shoulder patches.

When the attack began, the Roer itself threatened to be the main enemy. The rapid current pulled the assault boats downstream anywhere from 75 to 150 yards beyond their planned landing points. This not only complicated attack plans but disrupted the schedules of follow-up companies

Crouching in a shell hole, an infantryman of the U.S. Ninth Army awaits his turn to cross a footbridge over the Roer, after the turbulent river had subsided. In addition to a life belt and full pack, he is carrying two field pouches of extra ammunition and rations because supply deliveries across the swollen river were bound to be slow for several days.

that had to use the same boats in shuttles. Sometimes the current sent a boat swirling in circles and crashing into a partially completed bridge.

The river also played havoc with bridge-building efforts. At one site, the fast-running waters swamped 20 or so of the 450-pound pontoons on which a footbridge was supposed to rest, forcing the engineers to start all over again. A bridge at another site was so buffeted by the current after it was completed that it proved too unsteady for use. Two other bridges that the engineers managed to secure on the opposite shore met with trouble of a different kind. One took a misplaced round of artillery fire from the American side; the anchor line was cut, the abutment crumbled and the pneumatic floats on which the bridge rested were punctured. The other bridge was found to have a disconcerting object protruding from the ground athwart its exit point on the far side—an unexploded 500-pound bomb that an Allied plane had dropped sometime in the past. Both bridges were unusable for a time.

But none of these problems proved significant. Armored amphibious carriers and assault boats were on hand to supplement the bridges the engineers were struggling to throw across the Roer. By nightfall, two and a half divisions—nearly 25,000 American infantrymen—were across the river. Except for two first-wave companies that sustained 75 casualties in a woods studded with booby traps and antipersonnel mines, the Americans counted their losses as minimal; enemy resistance was no more than light to moderate. On the second day, the water level of the Roer had dropped enough to permit the construction of 19 bridges, seven of them vehicular. By the end of the third day, February 25, the Ninth Army held a salient six miles wide and three and a half miles deep to the north of the crossing area; the First Army held another bridgehead of roughly equal size to the south.

From these new positions beyond the broken barrier of the Roer, two vital moves were now possible. The northern salient led to the long-delayed linkup of Operation *Grenade* with Operation *Veritable;* the southern salient opened the way for a drive by First Army forces toward Cologne.

The implications were not lost on the venerable commander in chief of all German forces in the West, 69-year-old Field Marshal Gerd von Rundstedt. On February 25, even as General Simpson and General Hodges were preparing to expand their bridgeheads east of the Roer, Rundstedt appealed to Hitler for new directives. His message was one of unvarnished gloom: The entire Western Front would be in danger of coming apart unless his troops were allowed to retreat across the Rhine.

Receiving no response, Rundstedt tried again the next day. He begged to be allowed at least to withdraw troops from the so-called Roermond triangle north of Simpson's newly won northern salient. Part of General Schlemm's First Parachute Army was in the Roermond area and now stood in danger of being trapped. Rundstedt's second appeal to Hitler was answered. On February 27, the Führer refused to sanction even the minor tactical adjustment Rundstedt had suggested. Instead, he ordered a holding action, with units in the area to be "redeployed." A single curt sentence in the same message took note of Rundstedt's appeal of February 25: "Withdrawal behind the Rhine is unthinkable."

Desperate, Rundstedt made bold to repeat his request for the Roermond withdrawal. This time he won support. At a briefing for Hitler, the deputy chief of the Wehrmacht's operations staff command urgently endorsed the proposal. On February 28, Hitler approved, though "with a heavy heart," as he put it. But several days later, at an Armed Forces High Command (OKW) conference, the Führer was still fuming, ridiculing Rundstedt's persistent proposals for withdrawal and vowing that the aged field marshal would have to be "cured" of the idea of retreat. "These people just don't have any vision," said Hitler. Then, suddenly, came a flash of truth. Withdrawal, the Führer declared, "would only mean moving the catastrophe from one place to another."

His Allied foes could not have summed up the situation more accurately.

THE ORDEAL ON THE ROER

Infantrymen of the U.S. Ninth Army dash across Germany's Roer River on a footbridge that was constructed by combat engineers under intense enemy fire.

A PITCHED BATTLE ON AN ANGRY RIVER

In the early-morning darkness of February 23, 1945, several thousand combat engineers of the U.S. Ninth Army braced themselves for what they knew would be one of the sternest tests of the War: the crossing of the Roer River, the first major watercourse blocking the advance into Germany. The Germans were well dug in on the opposite bank; they had destroyed all the Roer bridges and had opened the giant Schwammenauel Dam upstream, turning the normally placid river into a churning torrent. The engineers had paused until the flood crest had passed, but now they could wait no longer. For behind them stood 14 full divisions impatient to leap the Roer and thrust on to the Rhine itself, 25 miles to the east.

At exactly 3:30 a.m., after a thunderous artillery bombardment, the engineers pushed out into the river aboard assault boats loaded with bridging equipment. With them came infantry vanguards intent on clearing the far shore of enemy troops. The first wave of boats reached the east bank with relative ease. But as the infantrymen fanned out, German gunners concentrated deadly mortar and machine-gun fire on the exposed engineers, who were struggling to ferry ropes and steel cables to anchor their pontoon footbridges.

At almost every crossing, engineers were shot out of their bobbing craft. And the river took a heavier toll than German marksmen. Boats slammed together in the current and crashed against bridges and floating debris. A battle report told how two boats of engineers and infantrymen came to grief. "One boat capsized and the other was caught by the current and washed downstream 350 yards. The men landed and tried to work their way south along the riverbank, but they ran into barbed wire and a minefield. Lieutenant Howland and several others were injured."

By the end of the first day, the small force of engineers had lost 31 men killed and 226 wounded—nearly one third of the entire Ninth Army's casualties that day. But they worked on, and within four days they had thrown almost two dozen bridges across the Roer, enough to transport 378,000 troops with all their equipment.

Using a guideline to brace against the dangerous current, a combat engineer carries bridging supplies to comrades waiting on the opposite shore.

An engineer, securing cables on a nearly completed pontoon footbridge, gets a helping hand from a buddy in an assault boat anchored near the far shore.

Infantrymen of the U.S. 29th Division hurry across a footbridge over the Roer as the rising sun shines through a shell-gutted house near the Aldenhoven roa

OOTING OUT SNIPERS
T THE BRIDGEHEADS

e combat engineers fought many a skir-
ish in the Roer assault. After crossing the
ormy river, the engineers joined infantry
sault teams to root out snipers and to
otect the work on the bridges.

One such action, part of which is shown
 this page, took place while the bridge
 left was being built. Men of the 121st
gineer Battalion cornered some snipers
ght) in the woods near the road to Al-
nhoven. After trading shots, the Ger-
ans surrendered (below). Suddenly one
isoner threw a grenade into the middle
 the group. The blast wounded two engi-
ers and the photographer, and killed the
erman who had thrown the grenade.

Scouting the eastern bank of the Roer,
an engineer patrol edges toward a few snipers
trapped between two American crossings.

fles at the ready, combat engineers march their prisoners back to the river. One German anxiously keeps waving a white handkerchief to signal surrender.

On a footbridge near Jülich, stretcher-bearers carry a wounded engineer shoreward, stepping over the crumpled corpse of a GI.

A DESPERATE DRAMA ON THE SPAN AT JÜLICH

The engineers' most harrowing struggle to cross the Roer came at the town of Jülich. German troops observing from an ancient citadel perched on an inland height used radios to direct the gunfire of their comrades, enabling them to destroy one bridge, as shown in these pictures.

The engineers who were trying to build another bridge at Jülich were repeatedly thwarted. They had no sooner strung a guideline across the river than it was severed by an exploding mortar shell. A second line snagged in the swirling debris and snapped. The third line was cut by another shellburst that wounded three men. On their fourth attempt, the engineers managed to construct 48 feet of bridge—but then the swift current that had been tearing at the pontoons snapped the cables, and the bridge collapsed.

After nearly 16 hours, the engineers' persistence paid off. On their fifth try, they completed the bridge, and it stayed up. Men, guns and supplies streamed across.

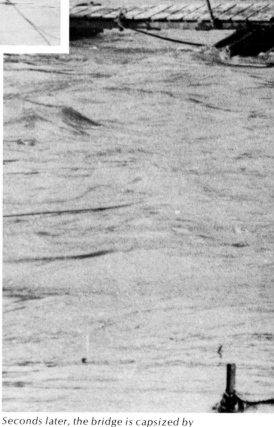

Seconds later, the bridge is capsized by a shellburst. The stretcher-bearers struggle to keep the wounded man from being swept away. On the shore, soldiers watch helplessly.

Engineers in an assault boat rescue the stretcher-bearers and the wounded engineer. The dead man, covered by enemy guns, was left on the broken bridge until nightfall.

A reminder of the cost of victory, a U.S. Army engineer lies dead beneath the guidelines of a pontoon bridge on the Roer. Many of the dead were washed downstream, and their bodies were never recovered.

Looking more like the debris of defeat than a symbol of success, the expendable assault boats cast adrift by the first U.S. troops to cross the Roer join the wreckage of a bridge dynamited by the Germans.

MOPPING UP BEFORE HEADING FOR THE RHINE

Within one day of the initial assault, the Roer crossing was a tactical success, and the Ninth Army's vanguard was moving northeast toward the Rhine. But the engineers stayed behind to build more bridges, bury the dead and police the bridgehead.

In the aftermath of the operation, the riverbanks were littered with abandoned boats, sections of broken bridges and other battle debris. The engineers had thrown the first bridges across the Roer with little regard for the barbed-wire entanglements and minefields strewn along the banks. But now, as more and heavier bridges spanned the river, the engineers toiled to clear out the deadly mines that seemed to be everywhere.

When the work was done, the engineers faced another job: They headed northeast to perform the same feats on an even grander scale on the banks of the Rhine.

2

As the Allied armies drew closer to the Rhine, Adolf Hitler's orders to his commanders on the west bank betrayed a significant shift in his thinking. Though his earlier instructions to hold firm still stood, it was clear that he had begun to accept the inevitability of a retreat across the river. For Hitler to have admitted as much would have been out of character. But the new orders issuing from the Reich Chancellery in Berlin were increasingly concerned with what was to be done—and not done—in the event that a withdrawal across the Rhine became necessary.

Accustomed as they were to the Führer's often-confusing directives, the German commanders found this latest batch even more baffling than usual. One order specified that Hitler's explicit permission would be required before even one soldier or one piece of equipment could be evacuated from the west bank to the east; yet the very mention of evacuation was a portent. Other orders concerned the bridges over the Rhine. Hitler made it plain that they were to be destroyed before they could fall into Allied hands; one directive advised that anyone who failed to do so in time would be summarily executed. But, he added, the same fate would await anyone who blew up a bridge too soon.

The ticklish task of deciding precisely the right or wrong moment to destroy a bridge was left to each area commander—along with the personal responsibility for the outcome. At least one commander—the First Parachute Army's General Schlemm—was able to find some macabre humor in this dilemma. Schlemm, whose forces along the northern front represented the heaviest concentration of German strength on the west bank, later told an American interrogator: "Since I had nine bridges in my sector, I could see my hopes for a long life rapidly dwindling."

The Allies, for their part, had little doubt that the bridges would be blown before they could be seized; it was inconceivable that the methodical Germans would fail in so crucial a matter. It was on this assumption that the Allied plans for the Rhine crossing were based. The attacking armies would have to cross the river on their own—in boats and on bridges built by their own engineers.

From first to last, it would be a stupendous undertaking. Simply assembling the armada of boats and the bridge-building materials would pose a logistical challenge unequaled since the Normandy invasion. Eisenhower himself

THE RACE FOR THE BRIDGES

saw a similarity between the two operations. The Rhine crossing, he said, "resembled an assault against a beach, except that the troops, instead of attacking from ship to shore, were carried into the battle from shore to shore."

The supply effort had been under way since December and had taken longer than expected—in no small part because of the disruptions caused by the Battle of the Bulge. A prodigious assortment of items had to be collected: preassembled bridge sections, cranes, pontoons, outboard motors. A number of heavy anchors for pontoon bridges were purchased from Belgian barge owners who were more than happy to help in the fight against the former occupiers of their homeland. Belgian factories in Brussels and Antwerp supplied miles of steel cable, and special pile-driving hammers were designed and manufactured to satisfy the demand for fixed bridges.

By February, the Allies' rivergoing fleet had grown to 2,780 craft of every shape and description. Some were brought in on northern Europe's waterways. Others came overland by road. For this purpose, special trailers were constructed to transport boats that were as large as 50 feet long and 14 feet wide.

The British Royal Navy and the U.S. Navy provided personnel to man the larger craft and trained the assault troops to operate the smaller boats. "What the hell are you guys doing so far from the ocean?" a surprised corporal asked on running into a fellow American in a sailor's uniform. "We're gonna take you landlubbers across the Rhine!" came the reply.

The planners tried to anticipate every eventuality—even such a wildly improbable event as a sweep up the Rhine by German U-boats; to fend off any such attack, antisubmarine and antimine booms were to be installed at crossing points. There were ingenious solutions to a number of unexpected problems. Engineers cutting thousands of logs for bridge pilings found that shell fragments deeply embedded in some trees were breaking the blades of the saws; a bright lad thought of employing mine detectors to locate the trouble spots. The British made a vital contribution to the planning effort by figuring out a way to transform the standard Sherman tank into an amphibious vehicle. The bottom of the hull was waterproofed and the tank's sides were fitted with canvas walls, which provided enough displacement to

make the tank float; propulsion was provided by twin propellers fitted to the tank engine.

A fundamental problem confronting the Allies was the choice of suitable crossing sites. For much of its length the Rhine was lined with rocky crags and steep hills; the careful technical preparations would prove of little avail if the men and the armor were halted by difficult terrain on the far side. After studying aerial photographs and intelligence reports, the officers planning the main thrust in the northern sector settled on three sites opposite a relatively level 20-mile stretch of the east bank with the small city of Wesel as the principal focus.

Aside from the topographical advantages, Wesel itself was well worth the taking. The Germans had turned it into a major communications center. Moreover, it served as a conduit for the shipment of coal and steel from the Ruhr district to the rest of Germany; barges from the Ruhr traveled down the Rhine to Wesel and branched off there into the Lippe Lateral Canal before finally entering the Dortmund-Ems Canal, which ran northward for 165 miles to Emden on the North Sea. Hitler now had more need of the Ruhr's coal and steel than ever before; Upper Silesia, which was his second-largest source of supply, was being overrun by the Russians. Wesel had therefore become a prize of enormous strategic importance; the specter of its seizure by the Allies had loomed large in Hitler's exhortations to hold the west bank at whatever cost.

By late February of 1945, General Schlemm and his First Parachute Army had considerably less of the west bank to defend than they had at the start of the month. British and Canadian forces were now in control of the towns of Cleves and Goch, nearly midway to the Rhine from Operation Veritable's jump-off point at Nijmegen. Schlemm's forces, 15 understrength divisions in all, had been squeezed into an area about 10 miles deep and 15 miles wide, roughly triangular in shape, with the apex at Xanten and the base extending southwestward from Kalkar.

The German situation was untenable, and Schlemm was well aware of it. The British and Canadians had vastly superior numbers: some 500,000 troops to fewer than 100,000 Germans, and 500 tanks to Schlemm's 50 panzers. Moreover, the British and Canadians would be augmented by

U.S. Ninth Army forces moving up from the south after the end of the long delay in crossing the Roer River. Nevertheless, the tenacious and thoroughly professional Schlemm was determined that the enemy would be made to pay for every inch of ground.

Local construction crews were conscripted to strengthen the First Parachute Army's defenses guarding the Wesel bridgehead. Three successive trench systems, about 500 yards apart, were dug along the approaches from the west and north. The open stretches between them were sown with wooden mines impervious to metal detectors. A network of knee-high barbed-wire entanglements was laid down to bedevil the advancing enemy infantry. Short on heavy artillery, Schlemm made a decision that he did not bother to clear with Berlin. From a sector of the West Wall, Schlemm stripped 50 high-velocity 88mm guns—normally reserved for antiaircraft duty—to use as superbly effective antitank weapons.

The countryside that Schlemm prepared to defend was a picture-book landscape dotted with villages, hamlets, pastures and wood lots, and laced with streams and canals. All but a few of the rises were gentle, and the view from observation points throughout the area was generally unimpeded. The best features of the terrain, from a defense standpoint, were two small adjoining forests, the Hochwald and the Balbergerwald, situated on high ground about five miles west of the Rhine and roughly parallel to it. It was here that Schlemm had concentrated his newly acquired 88s, and it was here, on the forward slopes of the high ground, that he had laid out his three-part trench system.

The attackers would have a difficult fight even before they arrived at the main Hochwald and Balbergerwald defenses. To the west and north lay a five-mile-long crescent of relatively high ground. The attackers would have to capture this high ground first, along with the German-held towns of Kalkar and Udem.

By way of paying homage to Germany's great 19th Century military theoretician, Field Marshal Alfred von Schlieffen, Schlemm dubbed his defense setup the "Schlieffen position." The British and the Canadians would remember it in their own terms as the "Hochwald layback," the last effective defense line west of the Rhine.

The mission of destroying this final obstacle on the way to the Rhine in the north was assigned by Field Marshal Montgomery to the Canadian First Army, commanded by Lieut. General Henry D. G. Crerar. The operation was code-named *Blockbuster,* signaling the intention to blast a great hole in Schlemm's defenses and barrel straight through. Before long, the name would become an embarrassing misnomer. Montgomery, who had seen the flower of German fighting men in action in the deserts of North Africa, was later to write that in the lower Rhineland "the enemy parachute troops fought with a fanaticism unexcelled at any time in the War."

The attack on the Kalkar-Udem ridge began two hours before dawn on February 26, spearheaded by the 2nd and 3rd Divisions of the Canadian II Corps under Lieut. General G. G. Simonds. A 600-gun bombardment preceded the troops, and "artificial moonlight"—searchlights reflecting off the low-hanging clouds—guided their advance.

By dawn on the 27th, the scene on the ridge south of Kal-

Wearing a welder's face mask, an American infantryman of the 26th Division uses an acetylene torch to complete a crossbow designed for hurling grenades great distances. He built the weapon as a pastime during the wait to cross the Rhine in February 1945.

In the attack plan for the Hochwald defenses, code-named Blockbuster, two Canadian infantry divisions were to seize Kalkar and Udem and the ridge between the two towns. This accomplished, the Canadian 4th Armored Division was to breach the gap along the railway between the Hochwald and the Balbergerwald and then, followed by the infantry, sweep eastward to Xanten.

kar testified to hand-to-hand combat of a terrible savagery. Bullet-riddled and bayoneted bodies, Canadian and German, lay everywhere, along with discarded flamethrowers some of the attackers had used to flush out the defenders. The Canadians had matched the foe in their ferocity. As one Allied chronicler of the battle put it, "The idea that the only way to end the War was to kill the Germans in front of them had struck home."

At the height of the battle, Sergeant Aubrey Cosens and four men of the Queen's Own Rifles of Canada, all that remained of their platoon, found themselves pinned down by intense German fire. Just then a Canadian tank arrived on

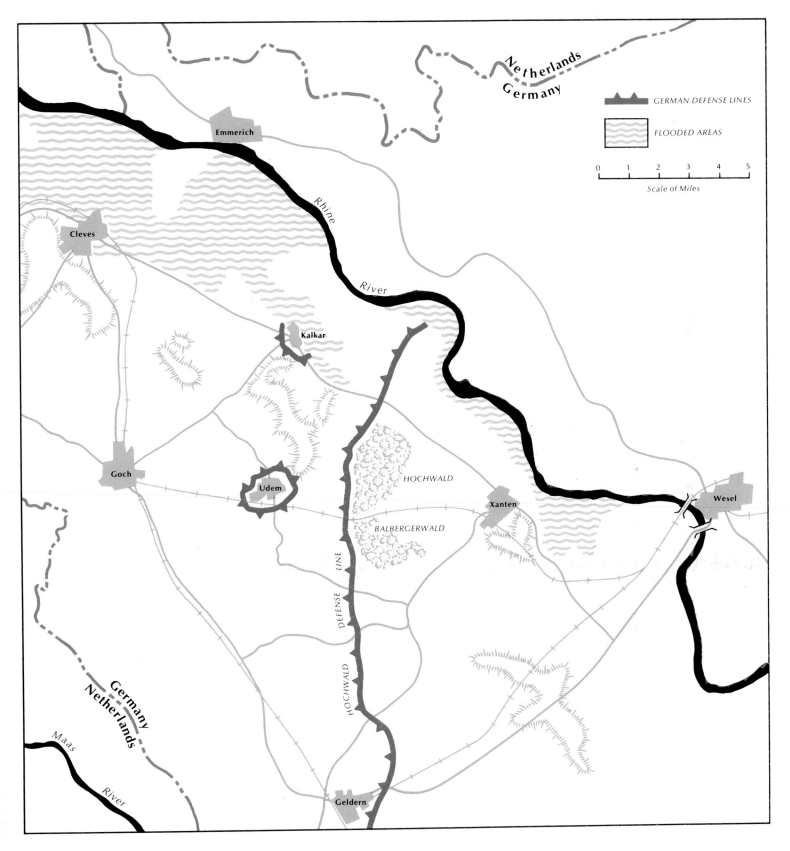

GERMAN DEFENSE LINES

FLOODED AREAS

Scale of Miles

the scene, and Cosens sprinted through a hail of bullets, clambered up onto the turret and directed the gunners' fire against the enemy positions. As the Germans counterattacked, the Canadians picked them off. Cosens then ordered the tank to smash into several farm buildings to rout the remaining Germans, whom he also helped to pick off. All told, Cosens personally killed 20 of the enemy and forced another 20 to surrender before he fell victim to a sniper's bullet while en route to company headquarters to report that the position had been captured. He was posthumously awarded the Victoria Cross, the British Commonwealth's highest award for valor.

Nevertheless, it took the Canadians six days, until March 3, to secure the Kalkar end of the ridge. Meanwhile, at Udem on the opposite end, the fighting had proved decisive earlier. By late afternoon on February 27, the Canadians held the town, and two regiments of the Canadian 4th Armored Division—the Algonquins and the 29th Armored Reconnaissance—were moving down the east-facing slope toward the gap between the Hochwald and the Balbergerwald. But as the Canadians fought their way across antitank ditches and minefields, the Germans put down a withering volume of fire from south, east and north. The Canadians got to within 500 yards of the gap, and then were pinned down—unable to move for 24 hours.

To *Blockbuster's* commander, General Simonds, the gap was the key to the swift success of his operation. Running through it, on an embanked roadbed, was a railway; in peacetime it had carried passengers and freight between the towns of Goch and Xanten. Now Goch was a staging point for Simonds' troops, and Xanten, as a gateway to Wesel across the river, was his ultimate objective. Simonds intended to have his engineers remove the tracks from the Goch-Xanten railway and then to use the roadbed as a highway for his men, armor and supplies.

The Canadians fought for the gap without respite for six desperate days and nights. A single battalion of Schlemm's paratroops, supported by heavy mortars and the fearsome 88s, contested every step of the way. Wedged inside the narrow corridor, the antagonists battled at a distance of only a few yards; attack and counterattack merged into one.

In the surrounding forests, the fighting also raged without pause. By night, Canadian positions were infiltrated time and again. German paratroopers would loom suddenly out of the darkness, lobbing grenades, firing machine pistols, jabbing and slashing with bayonets, and then fade back into the gloom. Schlemm's men had no need of maps to acquaint them with the terrain.

As Simonds' troops struggled to move forward, individual acts of valor were increasingly required and automatically performed. North of the gap in the Hochwald, Major Frederick A. Tilston of the Canadian 2nd Division's Essex Scottish Regiment took Company C across 500 yards of open ground and through a 10-foot swath of barbed wire to grapple with the Germans in their formidable triple-trench system. As he raced forward, he was grazed in the head by German fire. He leaped into the enemy defenses, flinging a grenade to silence a machine gun that was cutting down his men. Tilston dashed on, leading Company C to the second line of trenches another 500 yards away. He was now severely wounded in the thigh. Still he fought on, and in a desperate melee with clubbed weapons, knives and bare fists, the Essex cleared the second trench line. But before they could consolidate their gain, the Germans counterattacked behind a barrage of mortar and machine-gun fire.

By now Company C had lost more than 100 men. Tilston calmly moved about despite his painful wounds, encouraging his depleted forces and organizing a defense. Six times he crossed open ground under fire, carrying grenades and ammunition to his hard-pressed riflemen. Then he suffered a third hit in his other leg. Sprawled in a shell crater, he would not accept any medical aid until he had carefully instructed his one remaining officer on how to hold the company's position. Tilston's courage cost him both legs, and earned him the Victoria Cross.

On March 2, an event that was to help speed the end of Operation *Blockbuster* took place about nine miles south of the Hochwald gap, near the town of Geldern. The area that surrounded Geldern was part of *Blockbuster's* supporting southern flank, assigned to the British XXX Corps. Early that morning, Squadron A of the 4th / 7th Dragoon Guards was moving through the outskirts of the town when suddenly, from about 400 yards away, some tanks opened fire—American tanks. A British officer gingerly began walking toward the tanks holding up a recognition panel—a large cloth sheet, brightly colored so as to be visible at about half a mile, and more often used to identify ground troops to friendly aircraft.

The tanks belonged to a motorized task force of the 35th Division, U.S. Ninth Army. The 35th and a combat unit of the 8th Armored Division had driven 30 miles north from the Roer River area to effect the long-delayed linkup that had been planned to entrap Schlemm's forces.

But the wily Schlemm was too quick. Under cover of darkness that night, he began withdrawing his troops, skillfully masking his movements with intensified covering fire and counterattacks by rear-guard units. Gradually, over the next three days, the Canadians in the gap found a slack-ening of enemy resistance; as their advance continued, they were able to clear the surrounding forests as well. By March 6 they had broken through to the eastern end of the gap. The German defenders had vanished, leaving behind only their dead.

With the consent of his superiors in the high command of Army Group H, Schlemm had already prepared the position for his last stand on the west bank. The chosen area was almost in sight of the Rhine, and centered on Xanten. Within this shrunken perimeter Schlemm had strengthened every strong point, natural and man-made. The road leading to Xanten from the enemy-held northwest was cratered and mined, and was guarded by heavy concentrations of anti-

Caught in the light of parachute flares dropped by a British reconnaissance plane, orderly columns of retreating German convoys are seen streaming under a railroad viaduct near Duisburg, Germany, on the night of March 3, 1945. Despite such photo intelligence, Allied fighter-bombers were prevented by generally bad weather from striking at the retreating Germans, who succeeded in moving tens of thousands of men to the east bank of the river.

tank artillery and machine-gun nests. The town itself was strongly held by infantry and antitank forces.

The battle for Xanten began on March 6 and quickly proved to be a replica of the savage contest for the Hochwald layback. Schlemm's paratroopers and tankers fought with the desperate fury of men with their backs to the wall. Facing them were three Canadian and two British divisions well aware of the importance of their mission in the larger scheme of the war. The Americans were attacking from the south and as the German perimeter contracted, each Allied division had no more than about 1,000 yards of front; the foes were literally locked in combat.

Schlemm, realistic as ever, knew that his position was too small to be held for long; the larger Allied forces would soon be able to maneuver around it. He saw no practical reason to sacrifice the First Parachute Army west of the Rhine. Across the river, his experienced men could stiffen the 40,000 to 50,000 German replacement soldiers now on the east bank, thus offering a reasonable hope for developing an effective defense.

General Schlemm's view found a responsive audience among his superiors in Army Group H. But, of course, Berlin would have to be sounded out and that was a job for the commander in chief of Army Group H, General Johannes Blaskowitz. At Blaskowitz' personal request, the High Command at Hitler's headquarters dispatched a staff lieutenant colonel to verify Schlemm's assessment of the situation. As it happened, the emissary was more at home behind a desk than in the crucible of combat. Schlemm gave the nervous staff man one look at the bloodletting under way, and sent him back to Berlin. No further persuasion was necessary.

In fact, Schlemm's confidence in the outcome of the visit was such that he had already begun the evacuation on his own. While a powerful rear-guard action held the Canadians and British at bay, he kept a steady stream of troops moving through the bridgehead to the safety of the far side of the Rhine. Augmenting the nine bridges in his sector with makeshift ferries and small boats, and stationing his personal staff officers at the crossing sites to supervise, Schlemm managed a miracle of sorts. Along with the troops went supply units and administrative personnel, field trains, hospital equipment, stores of ammunition, and trucks carrying ma-chinery from factories and workshops on the west bank. A combination of antiaircraft guns massed at both ends of the bridges, bad weather and night movement enabled Schlemm to pull it off; something like 50,000 vehicles made it across the river by the morning of March 7.

At that point, Schlemm started blowing the bridges. By March 9, seven of the nine spans in his sector had been blown; only the two at Wesel remained. Schlemm had set up a special bridge command, with specified officers in charge of each bridge and demolition teams to do the necessary. A radio network tied the bridges to Schlemm's headquarters so he could personally issue the order to demolish. In light of Hitler's edict against destroying a bridge either too soon or too late, Schlemm's timing was faultless.

Throughout the night of March 9, Schlemm got the last of his surviving troops, and his scant remaining armor and heavy weapons, across the Rhine. All that was left behind was a small rear guard. At 7:00 a.m. on March 10, British troops now in control of Xanten heard the roar of two tremendous explosions off to the east: Both Wesel bridges, one a railway bridge, had been blown. Schlemm was later to say that it was the best way he knew of announcing the end of the battle.

At Xanten, Colonel John O. E. Vandeleur of the 4th Somerset Light Infantry added his own finishing touch. As the captured German paratroopers marched through town on their way to prisoner-of-war cages in the rear, Vandeleur and his staff stood in respectful silence, saluting. The incident raised a howl of public protest when reported in the Allied press, but Vandeleur stoutly defended his gesture: "The German garrison of Xanten," he said, "were very gallant men."

Throughout the course of Operation *Blockbuster*, General Simpson's U.S. Ninth Army had been making giant strides in the sector just to the south. With the crossing of the Roer River, after two frustrating weeks of waiting for its floodwaters to subside, the pent-up energies of the Americans burst forth in a spectacular sweep toward the Rhine.

On March 1, as troops of Simpson's XVI Corps were on their way to link up with *Blockbuster*, units of his XIII Corps closed in on the nearby city of Krefeld, less than five miles from the Rhine. At the same time, a division of his XIX Corps reached and took the city of München Gladbach, while spearheads of the XIX Corps stood on the west bank itself, near a city called Neuss. Altogether, the advance from the Roer had covered some 50 miles.

Simpson had expected that cities the size of Krefeld and München Gladbach would have to be enveloped, reduced, and perhaps even besieged; his staff had planned accordingly. But no such time-consuming efforts were needed. In contrast to the fierce fight put up by Schlemm's paratroopers to the north, the German defenders in this area, elements of the Fifth Panzer Army and a few other infantry units, simply faded away or opted to surrender. München Gladbach, a once-bustling textile center of 126,000 people, took only 24 hours to clear—and a single infantry regiment did the job.

On the night of the capture, Time-Life correspondent Sidney Olson joined some of the soldiers as they went searching for snipers. "The city lay mackerel dead," Olson reported. "The GIs made their way casually from house to house while the stolid German families sat quietly in their bunk-furnished, candle-lit air-raid basements, their children and old folks about them."

Moving from block to block, Olson and his companions occasionally came upon German soldiers in the street, still holding their rifles but standing stock still and offering no resistance. "The moment they saw you," Olson wrote, "they would put the rifles on the sidewalk and march up to surrender. The weary GIs would merely tell them to stand there, and would go on mopping up. As a result, there were Germans who surrendered literally scores of times before someone had time to take them off to a battalion command post. Some stood for hours; others wandered off in disgust."

At Neuss, nine miles due east, Simpson had a problem of a different sort. Across the Rhine lay the great Ruhr city of Düsseldorf, a temptingly near target, yet a potentially disastrous undertaking. The area around Düsseldorf, like much of the rest of the Ruhr, was a densely built-up industrial complex in which an attacking army might well bog down fighting for every factory, mill and railyard. Simpson knew that was why Eisenhower's battle plan had excluded a frontal assault on the Ruhr district. Instead, it was to be sealed inside a mammoth pocket formed by twin enveloping movements from north and south. And in the north, Montgomery was by no means ready to make this move.

Still, Simpson saw no harm in starting to slice away at the edges of the Ruhr—if he could get his forces across the river fast, before the Germans had a chance to destroy the eight bridges in his zone.

On the night of March 2, attempts were made to seize two of the bridges, and came agonizingly close to succeeding. Several American tanks of the 2nd Armored Division were actually clanking across the bridge at Ürdingen when the Germans blew it. The second bridge, at Oberkassel, was the object of a daring American ruse that the Germans discovered barely in time.

The scheme drew its inspiration from the ancient stratagem of the Trojan Horse: A task force of the 83rd Division was to disguise itself as a German column, pass unnoticed through the Germans, and snatch the bridge from under their very noses.

The deception had to take into account tanks as well as men. Since the American M4 tanks lacked the muzzle brakes of most German tanks, ammunition tubes were cut up and taped to the end of the Shermans' guns to represent

Helmeted soldiers of the U.S. Ninth Army and Canadian First Army troops in berets join forces near Geldern, Germany, on March 3, 1945, completing a linkup that would, in the words of one correspondent, "squeeze the Germans like paste through a tube."

the foot-long ventilated cylinders the Germans used on their guns to reduce recoil. The white-star insignia on the turrets of the American tanks was hidden beneath a coat of olive-drab paint and, as on the German tanks, large identification numbers were printed on the forward turret slope. German crosses were painted on the hull. Somebody also remembered that the American buggy-whip tank radio antenna was far more prominent than the stumpy German rod antenna. Since the task force was to move in radio silence, the buggy whips could be tied down.

The operation commenced in the darkness of March 2. The men wore long field-gray overcoats and helmets provided from captured German stores. They moved in a column of threes, in the German manner, rather than in twos, American style. German-speaking GIs were placed in front of the tanks to do any talking that might be required; the rest of the formation marched beside and behind the tanks, as the Germans did.

Tank engines rumbling, the task force gained the main road to Oberkassel without incident and swung down the blacktop. Strict discipline prevailed: There was no smoking and no talking except for muttered "Heil Hitlers" as the Americans passed German outposts. At one point, some German troops marched down one side of the road while the Americans moved along the other side. The U.S. task force reached Oberkassel without a shot being fired.

But as dawn lightened the sky, a German soldier on a bicycle paused, scanned the task force with obvious suspicion and sped off to sound the alarm. A shot by one of the Americans toppled him from his cycle—and ended the deception. The task force raced through Oberkassel just as the town's air-raid siren sounded. As the first American tanks arrived at the bridge, an explosion sent the structure crashing into the Rhine.

Simpson was undeterred. If he could not seize one of the Germans' bridges, he could stage a surprise crossing on a bridge built by his own engineers. He presented this proposal to Montgomery, under whose command he was still technically operating. As Simpson saw it, the time was right and the circumstances favorable. The east-bank defenses opposite him were weak, and he thought he could get a foothold in the Ruhr on the far side of the Rhine. But Montgomery, with his innate distaste for improvisation, vetoed the pro-

posal. The field marshal remained unshaken in his belief that a carefully prepared and coordinated assault on the Rhine was the only way to succeed.

At American command posts all along the west bank, the widespread annoyance with Montgomery was quickly offset by a stunning new U.S. coup in the zone just south of Simpson's: On March 6, General Hodges' First Army reached the great cathedral city of Cologne.

Hodges had been looking forward to the prospect for weeks. Since early February, when his forces had failed in their attempt to capture the Roer dams intact, the First Army had served, in effect, as an adjunct to Simpson's Ninth Army. It had waited with the Ninth for the Roer to recede; when the river was finally jumped, the First Army divisions that went across were primarily intended to guard the Ninth's southern flank. But with the Ninth's move north from its bridgehead to join Montgomery's forces, the First was free to exploit its own bridgehead—and Hodges was happy to turn the troops loose.

The timing was fortunate. Hodges' superior, General Bradley, had the responsibility for Operation Lumberjack, the drive across the center of the Allied front facing the Germans. But Lumberjack—by Eisenhower's order—was to begin only after Montgomery's forces reached the Rhine. That event took place in the final days of February. As of March 1, Lumberjack could begin, and Hodges—much to Bradley's delight—was destined to score the operation's first major triumph.

Within a few days of securing their salient east of the Roer, Hodges' men had slashed through light German op-

Cologne Cathedral, lofty centerpiece of a prosperous city before World War II (top left), was surrounded by bombed-out ruins when American troops entered the Rhineland capital on the 6th of March, 1945. A GI reported, "Hardly a street remained that was not pitted by giant craters or blocked by huge mountains of rubble. The city was paralyzed."

In front of his ruined shop, a Cologne merchant puts the finishing touches on a sign declaring "Pilfering Forbidden" after painting a skull and crossbones for added effect. The sign was directed mainly at war-weary Germans suddenly released from Nazi control. Life photographer Margaret Bourke-White reported that "looting was everybody's open and frank occupation" until the American authorities imposed a ban.

position to leap the Erft River farther eastward and gone racing over the Cologne plain. By March 5 they were roaring down on the city itself.

The attack by the First Army's VII Corps, under Major General J. Lawton "Lightning Joe" Collins, began with a tank charge against Cologne's airfield. The base was defended by 16 of the feared 88mm antiaircraft guns that could have been deadly to the rolling armor had they been manned by crews accustomed to firing at ground-level targets. As it was, the 88s were manned by Luftwaffe troops who were practiced only at tracking aircraft; they could not bring the guns to bear quickly enough on the troop-laden U.S. tanks as they rumbled out of a smoke screen and overran the defenses.

The field was in American hands by nightfall, after which Cologne's defenses crumbled. The next morning Collins' troops sped south and east through the city, bent on seizing the Hohenzollern Bridge across the Rhine. They were greeted by a thunderous roar that rattled their helmets and sent a spray of pigeons aloft from the twin spires of Cologne's 13th Century cathedral. German demolition crews had blown a 1,200-foot gap in the bridge.

For the American soldiers, Cologne was a first look at a full-fledged German metropolis—and a sobering look it was. More than 50,000 tons of bombs, dropped on the city in more than 160 Allied air strikes since the first 1,000-plane raid staged by Royal Air Force bombers in 1942, had achieved fearsome results.

Cologne, as one GI put it, was little more than a mass of "wrecked masonry surrounded by city limits." Block after block of dwellings, shops and offices and public buildings had been smashed as though by giant hammers. Mounds of rubble clogged main avenues as well as side streets. Trolley wires lay twisted on their poles. A sickening stench of decay hung in the air. The people—those who remained of the 800,000 peacetime inhabitants—all seemed to be living in cellars. One of the first things that struck the Americans about them was their pallor.

In their contacts with the conquerors, the citizens of Cologne seemed stunned, conciliatory and more than anxious to please. "You want jewelry?" a frightened *Hausfrau* asked a patrolling soldier, not certain of what to expect.

"Naw, keep it, I ain't no looter," the GI growled. "But you got any eggs? I'll take eggs."

There were no eggs. Among the city's civilians, any kind of food was at a premium, though Collins' troops uncovered evidence that Cologne's Nazi hierarchy had got along nicely. They found massive meat lockers crammed with beef, and Corporal Henry Lattorella came upon a huge underground storage system that contained enough brandy to have inebriated every one of the 350,000 or so men in the First Army.

There were more discoveries, grim and otherwise. Troops detailed to open up the notorious *Staats Gefängnis,* or State Prison, found 85 German inmates suffering from both starvation and typhus. The Third Reich had incarcerated them as "political enemies." In a private dwelling, Lieut. Colonel Morris Kezee flushed a resplendently uniformed German from a closet hiding place; he thought he had captured a German general at the very least, only to learn from First Army interrogators that the man was the city's chief trolley-car conductor.

Time-Life correspondent Olson went for a look at two of Cologne's best-known sights: the Gothic cathedral and the medieval *Rathaus* (city hall). Inside the cathedral, the great vaulted roof was almost intact. But the floor was littered with glass from the shattered windows and chunks of stone that had crumbled from the pillars as a result of the concussion of bombs falling nearby. A pair of GIs stood nervously fingering their M-1s at the sound of German sniper fire just beyond the walls. Trying to lighten the tension, Olson commented that this was one of the most famous buildings in the world. The GIs were not too impressed. "Ain't much of a place right now, is it?" one of them remarked.

At the *Rathaus,* Olson came upon traces of a more definitive expression of soldierly opinion. On the stairs in the lobby stood a granite pillar bearing bronze letters that read *Ein*

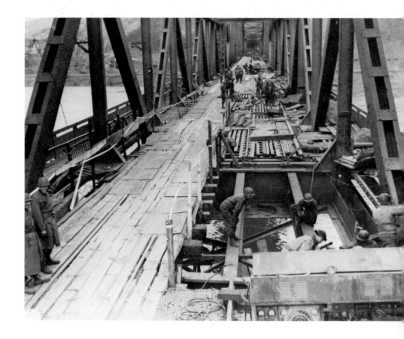

Seized by American troops on March 7, 1945, the Ludendorff Bridge at Remagen enabled the U.S. First Army to establish a strong foothold on the east bank of the Rhine. But the bridge had been seriously damaged by German demolition charges, and although American engineers (right) worked around the clock to make repairs, the weakened span collapsed (center and far right) into a mass of twisted rubble 10 days after its capture.

Volk, Ein Reich, Ein Führer (One People, One Germany, One Leader). For some years the top of the pedestal had held a bronze head of Hitler, but times had suddenly changed. As Olson put it: "Some GI had given the pillar a burst and had knocked off Hitler's head."

On March 7, a triumph of even greater psychological impact than the capture of a once-proud metropolis was scored by another First Army force, the III Corps, 30 miles south of Cologne. As part of the overall drive to the Rhine, a tank-infantry unit of the 9th Armored Division headed for the river near its junction with a tributary, the Ahr. At this point the Rhine flowed between steep bluffs; nestled at the foot of the gorge was the little town of Remagen, in prewar years a resort for health-conscious Germans who came to sip the waters of its mineral springs.

At about 1 p.m. on March 7, the task force reached a patch of woods above Remagen. Second Lieutenant Emmet J. Burrows, commanding the lead infantry platoon, slipped through the trees for a look at the Rhine. What he saw astonished him. At the southern edge of the town, a large railway bridge spanned the Rhine—and it was intact. The bridge—named Ludendorff in honor of Germany's revered World War I general—was more than 1,000 feet long, with two planked-over railroad tracks and footpaths on either side. German soldiers were streaming across to the east bank.

The word was flashed back, and Brigadier General William M. Hoge, a veteran engineer officer in charge of the task force, hurried forward. He found the troops already on the move, the infantry footing it down the bluffs and a platoon of five Pershing M26 tanks descending a narrow winding road. Hoge issued some quick orders for the men to race to the bridge and bypass any pockets of resistance.

A few hours later the infantry and the attached tank platoon, led by First Lieutenant Karl H. Timmermann of A Company, 27th Armored Battalion, had bulled through the town of Remagen against only token resistance. As they neared the western end of the bridge—marked by two massive stone towers blackened by locomotive soot—a thunderous blast rent the air and a geyser of rocks and dirt erupted in the Americans' path.

Timmermann thought at first that the bridge was gone. But as the dust settled, he saw that the explosion had merely gouged a 30-foot trench across the western approach to the bridge. The trench would deny the bridge to the American tanks—at least temporarily. But it would do nothing to deter the infantry.

Captain Karl Friesenhahn, the German engineer officer responsible for the bridge, had touched off this first set of charges on his own initiative. He now went running back across the span to get permission to destroy the bridge itself. He was partway across when the concussion from an exploding American tank shell knocked him unconscious. After 15 minutes he struggled to his feet, still dazed, and staggered on. By now the eastern end of the bridge was blanketed by the heavy white smoke from phosphorus shells fired by American tanks to blind and demoralize the German soldiers who remained on the span. Their screams, as the burning phosphorus seared their flesh, were clearly audible to the Americans.

On the east bank, Friesenhahn's superior, Captain Willi Bratge, had set up his command post inside a railway tunnel that had been bored through a massive hill of rock named the Erpeler Lei.

The tunnel was a bedlam. As American fire from across the river battered the entrance, cowering townspeople with their wailing children and their farm animals competed for cover with frightened soldiers and foreign slave laborers. The command situation was just as confused. Late that morning a Major Hans Scheller had arrived from the 67th

Corps with orders to take command of the bridge. Captain Bratge, who had been in charge of the bridge defenses since August 1944, at first suspected that Scheller was an impostor, and demanded identification. But Bratge was quickly convinced that Scheller was legitimate, and the two officers agreed to joint command.

When Captain Friesenhahn rushed into the tunnel, seeking immediate permission to blow the bridge, Bratge and Scheller shared a prudent thought: Their decision to destroy the bridge ought to be on the record. And so they had a lieutenant write down the exact wording of the destruction order and the time—3:20 p.m.

Bratge then conveyed the order to Friesenhahn, who in turn thought it might be a good idea—in the event of any future problems—if he got his orders in writing too. But then his common sense prevailed and he rushed to the demolition switch just inside the tunnel entrance. He turned the spring key that was supposed to activate the electrical circuitry and set off a second set of explosives. Nothing happened. Friesenhahn tried twice more—again without result.

The circuit was broken. Friesenhahn thought of putting a repair team to work, but there was no time to do the job that way. Instead, he called for a volunteer to run onto the bridge to ignite by hand a third emergency-demolition system. A Sergeant Faust stepped forward. Friesenhahn squatted at the edge of the bridge, watching anxiously as the sergeant, ducking and crouching to avoid U.S. shells and bullets, ran 80 yards across the bridge to the primacord fuse.

After what seemed hours to Friesenhahn, Faust started back at a run. Then came an ear-cracking roar as 650 pounds of high explosive went off. Wooden planks leaped wildly in the air. The bridge shuddered and seemed to rise, as if it were about to fly from its foundations. Hunched against the explosion, Friesenhahn sighed with relief—the job was done. When he looked again, however, the bridge was still there. The charge was only half as powerful as that needed to do the job.

From the bluffs on the west bank, General Hoge headed his jeep downhill to order the entire U.S. task force sent across the bridge at once. Though the explosion had ripped huge holes in the planking over the railroad tracks, the footpaths were still usable. Lieutenant Timmermann, the company commander, signaled his platoon leaders forward.

Working their way onto the bridge, the infantrymen gave a fair approximation of football broken-field running—dodging, weaving, darting from the cover of one steel girder to another. They kept moving in spite of the lethal spatter of machine-gun fire from the two bridge towers near the east bank and shellfire from the guns on the bank itself. The infantry's own weapons, augmented by the 90mm guns of the Pershing tanks on the American side, helped keep down the German fire.

Close behind the first infantrymen on the bridge followed a small task force of engineers, working swiftly to cut all wires that might lead to more demolition charges underneath the bridge deck. They used their carbines to shoot apart the main cable that controlled the demolitions. The engineers discovered 60 separate charges of explosives, and defused all of them.

At the far end—after running more than 300 yards under fire—several of Timmermann's men veered off to clear the machine gunners from the bridge towers, while others sped on to the east bank. The first man to set foot beyond the Rhine was Sergeant Alex A. Drabik, a lanky Ohioan who had lost his helmet on the way. Lieutenant Timmermann and several others were only seconds behind him. By a curious coincidence, Timmermann's father had marched across this very bridge as a member of the American Army of Occupation in Germany in 1919.

As the men spread out on the east bank and one platoon

Battle-weary Sergeant Alex A. Drabik, who was the first American to reach the east bank of the Rhine, pauses for an official photograph after leading the charge across the Ludendorff Bridge on March 7, 1945. Drabik became a celebrity by mistake; in the confusion of the charge, he sprinted over the bridge in search of his platoon leader—who was actually behind him and came across the river several minutes later.

began scaling the 627-foot-high Erpeler Lei to silence the artillery at the top, Major Scheller, inside the tunnel, tried time and again to contact the 67th Corps. However painful, it was Scheller's duty to report that the Ludendorff Bridge was still standing. Failing to reach headquarters, Scheller rode off on a bicycle to convey the word in person. As the Americans began to swarm into the tunnel, Captain Bratge, Captain Friesenhahn and their men surrendered. Not long afterward, a large lettered sign went up on the bridge. It read: CROSS THE RHINE WITH DRY FEET—COURTESY OF THE 9TH ARMORED DIVISION.

News of the triumph at Remagen quickly traveled up the line from divisional headquarters to the III Corps to the First Army commander. General Hodges telephoned General Bradley at Twelfth Army Group headquarters. Bradley could not contain his jubilation.

"Hot dog, Courtney," he shouted. "This will bust 'em wide open. Shove everything you can across!"

With Bradley at the time was Eisenhower's chief of planning and operations, General Bull—the officer who had sparked Bradley's angry outburst a few weeks earlier by proposing that he divert some of his divisions to another part of the front. Bull took a less enthusiastic view of the Remagen episode. Such a dispersion of Bradley's strength, he said, would interfere with Eisenhower's plan to make the main Allied effort north of the Ruhr.

Bradley turned uncharacteristically sarcastic. "What the hell do you want us to do," he snapped, "pull back and blow the bridge up?"

Later that night Bradley placed a telephone call to Eisenhower at Rheims, where the Supreme Allied Commander had established his forward headquarters. Eisenhower was at dinner when the call came through. Looking back on what he described as "one of my happy moments of the War," Eisenhower later recounted the conversation with Bradley in full detail:

"When he reported that we had a permanent bridge across the Rhine I could scarcely believe my ears. He and I had frequently discussed such a development as a remote possibility but never as a well-founded hope.

"I fairly shouted into the telephone: 'How much have you got in that vicinity that you can throw across the river?'

"He said, 'I have more than four divisions but I called you to make sure that pushing them over would not interfere with your plans.'

"I replied, 'Well, Brad, we expected to have that many divisions tied up around Cologne and now those are free. Go ahead and shove over at least five divisions instantly, and anything else that is necessary to make certain of our hold.'

"His answer came over the phone with a distinct tone of glee: 'That's exactly what I wanted to do but the question has been raised here about conflict with your plans, and I wanted to check with you.' "

Bradley's glee was understandable, and not only because General Bull, who had raised the question, was present to overhear Eisenhower's response. Bradley was well aware that the news of Remagen would soon reach Field Marshal Montgomery in the north. He also knew that Montgomery was not scheduled to cross the Rhine for another two weeks. In effect, Bradley had trumped his great rival's ace.

Eisenhower, too, had Montgomery in mind, and quickly telephoned him to stave off the objections he might have to diverting any forces at all to the new bridgehead. The field marshal surprised the Americans by expressing his delight over the outcome at Remagen. "It will undoubtedly be an unpleasant threat to the enemy," he said, "and will undoubtedly draw enemy strength onto it and away from the business in the north."

As it happened, the Ludendorff Bridge proved to be less permanent than Eisenhower had hoped. Once in American hands, it became a repeated target of German long-range artillery and Luftwaffe attacks; rubber-suited German frogmen, towing rafts loaded with explosives, made a futile attempt to demolish the bridge from below. Although the Germans failed to destroy the span, the already-damaged structure gradually weakened under the weight of U.S. traffic. After five days, the Americans stopped using it, crossing instead on treadway bridges their engineers had installed. The engineers continued to work on the Ludendorff, bent on repairing it for future use. But on March 17, ten days after it had served the Americans' primary purpose, the center of the span fell into the river, carrying several of the repair crewmen to their deaths.

Nevertheless, as General Bradley said, the bridgehead at Remagen remained an "open wound" in the enemy's side.

HOLLAND'S "HUNGER WINTER"

A young Dutch girl in The Hague digs headfirst in a garbage can, desperately searching for anything edible during the famine-stricken winter of 1944-1945.

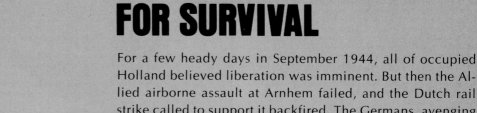

A FEARFUL STRUGGLE FOR SURVIVAL

For a few heady days in September 1944, all of occupied Holland believed liberation was imminent. But then the Allied airborne assault at Arnhem failed, and the Dutch rail strike called to support it backfired. The Germans, avenging the strike in the provinces they still held north of the Rhine and Waal Rivers, imposed a reign of terror on 4.5 million people—40 per cent of Holland's population.

The ports of Amsterdam and Rotterdam were wrecked by demolitions. More than 120,000 men were rounded up and sent to German labor camps. The Germans had been systematically commandeering food from the Dutch ever since the start of the Occupation. Now they stepped up their looting and clamped a virtual embargo on food shipments from the farmlands to the urban areas. Coal supplies, gas and electricity were also cut off. The German intent was clear: to starve and freeze the Dutch into submission.

In the hard-hit cities, the Dutch pinched and improvised to combat hunger and cold. Municipal kitchens, set up early in the War, fed as many people as possible with the meager food stocks at hand. Dutch officials in charge of food distribution were forced to reduce the daily ration from 1,500 calories in September to a starvation-level 900 in November, and then lower still. People foraged for extra food to survive, and to get wood to heat their homes they ripped apart abandoned buildings and deforested the landscape.

Conditions worsened steadily in the early months of 1945. Much of the population suffered from the swollen legs and faces of "hunger edema." The death rate climbed, and the early clamor of protest gave way to an eerie silence that one journalist explained succinctly: "Those who are hungry shout, but those who are starving keep still."

Not entirely still. The victims sent their government-in-exile in London secret messages begging for a relief army. But the Allies, committed to the invasion of Germany and fearing that an attack in Holland's north country would provoke the Germans into opening the dikes and flooding the lowlands, did not send help until late April. By then, it was too late for 18,000 men, women and children.

German troops, leaving the snowbound city of Amsterdam in March 1945, haul off wagonloads of food confiscated from the starving Dutch.

Gaunt-faced and spotted with malnutrition sores, an Amsterdam woman resolutely keeps up appearances, wearing earrings and her best hat. The Dutch women, one man recalled, were "the toughest and strongest, the ones who fought hardest for survival. Life revolved around them."

Striding out briskly in the bitter cold, two women wheel a cartload of goods they will use to barter for food in the hinterland miles outside of Amsterdam.

A couple of youths slip across a gangplank to steal sugar beets from a barge moored in Amsterdam. A friend of theirs on the quay keeps a sharp lookout.

FOOD THIEVES AND "HUNGER TRIPPERS"

Hunger, constant and almost unbearable, drove thousands of Dutch city dwellers to desperate measures. Parents sent their children out to steal; women sold themselves to German soldiers for a few cans of soup; rich and poor alike swarmed into the farmlands to search for food. Traveling on rickety bicycles or bleeding feet, the so-called hunger trippers trekked hundreds of miles to barter their watches or bed linens for some potatoes or eggs.

Most farmers tried to help, but some were hostile, scorning the "beggars" from the cities. And when the hunger trippers did find food it was often confiscated by a German patrol on the way home.

Amsterdam factory hands crowd around for a bowl of watery "stew"—mostly a smattering of vegetables, very rarely any meat. Its only merit was that it was h

Dutch policemen wait at a bakery for a consignment of bread that they will have to guard from thieves en route to a municipal kitchen in Rotterdam.

A DWINDLING DOLE FROM MUNICIPAL KITCHENS

Every morning in cities throughout occupied Holland, hungry, hollow-eyed people lined up by the thousands—350,000 in The Hague—for anything that the municipal kitchens could feed them. Henri A. van der Zee, who was 10 years old at the start of the winter of famine, later wrote, "My days were spent, for the most part, in queuing for whatever the ration cards promised us." It was so cold outside "that I still remember the tears of pain and misery turning to icicles on my cheeks."

Rations varied from city to city, depending upon what was available. In Rotterdam—for a while—each citizen was enti-

tled to a daily ration of 300 grams of potatoes, 200 grams of bread, 9 grams of fat, 28 grams of beans or peas and 5 grams of meat and cheese. "It was just too much to die on," one Rotterdamer recalled, "but certainly too little to keep you alive."

All too soon potatoes disappeared, to be replaced by sugar beets, a turnip-shaped root originally grown for its sugar content. The woody roots, which had to be thinly sliced and cooked to a pulpy mash, were a challenge to make edible. Van der Zee found the pulp "revoltingly mushy and sweet," but having no other choice he ate it "almost daily, retching in spite of my hunger." By April, even the supply of sugar beets had diminished, and each city dweller's ration had hit rock bottom—230 calories a day.

Solemn-faced children were seen everywhere carrying bowls and buckets in the hope of finding food. They were thin, wan, dirty and lice-ridden; some wer

arefoot. But they doggedly pressed their frigid search, often in vain. "They looked like little old men," an Amsterdamer said, "tough, defiant—and hungry."

Troops of a tank unit from the Canadian 5th Division hand out biscuits to a swarm of children in Putten, 64 miles northwest of Arnhem, in April 1945.

OPERATION "MANNA" FOR A STARVING PEOPLE

"It is already famine," Dutch food officials wired London on April 24; "in 10 days it will be death." In fact, the corpses of those who had died of starvation were already piling up in morgues and churches for the lack of coffins and able-bodied gravediggers. But help was finally on its way.

Canadian First Army troops had broken through into occupied Holland late in March and were advancing rapidly to the north. And on April 29, in a dramatic airlift that sent Dutch spirits soaring, RAF bombers began dropping precious "bombs" of food—flour, chocolate and egg powder —at sites near The Hague and Rotterdam. For those still strong enough to welcome the Allied planes, Operation Manna meant the long "Hunger Winter" was over.

ood packages fall—''like confetti from a giant hand,'' a reporter said—to be gathered up by relief workers at Amsterdam's Schipol Airport on May 3, 1945.

71

3

In Berlin, news of the Americans' seizure of the Remagen bridge set off a search for scapegoats. One convenient culprit was found at once: Field Marshal von Rundstedt. The Commander in Chief West was dealt with expeditiously.

On March 9, 1945, two days after the Remagen fiasco, Hitler summoned Rundstedt from his headquarters at Ziegenberg, decorated him with Germany's second-highest honor, the Swords of the Knight's Cross, and told him that he was being retired. The venerable field marshal, a hero in 1940 for his conduct of the blitzkrieg into France and the Low Countries, unobtrusively made his way to Upper Bavaria, where he was later taken prisoner by the Americans.

Hitler's choice to replace Rundstedt was Field Marshal Albert Kesselring, then commanding the German forces in northern Italy. Kesselring's reception at the Reich Chancellery on the same day was cordial and leisurely. For several hours, as Kesselring dutifully listened, Hitler discoursed on the German military situation in both east and west.

The War's outcome, Hitler explained, hinged on what happened on the Russian front, which therefore had priority. But once the Reich's eastern armies were reinforced, there would still be time to "refit the exhausted units" in the west. Though no fresh divisions were available, there would be a continuous flow of men and matériel, eventually bolstered by new jet fighters and "other novel weapons." Meanwhile, said Hitler, what was needed was a commander younger and more active than Rundstedt, someone who had both the confidence of the men in the line and experience in battling the Allies.

Kesselring was flattered and at the same time reluctant. He was still recuperating from a concussion suffered in Italy the previous October when his car collided with an artillery piece coming out of a side road. But his reputation for toughness had emerged intact; the joke among his troops after the accident was that the field marshal was doing well, but that the gun he hit had to be scrapped. Hitler wanted a general of such fiber, and Kesselring could not refuse.

The next day, addressing the assembled staff at Ziegenberg, Kesselring had a joke of his own, possibly inspired by Hitler's passing reference to novel weapons. For months, rumors had been circulating about a new "vengeance" weapon called the V-3, a monster successor to the V-1 buzz bombs and V-2 rockets that had been loosed against Lon-

"THE ENEMY CANNOT ESCAPE"

don. Supposedly the V-3—its exact nature was mysterious—was so powerful that it could turn the tide of war back in Germany's favor. But the dispirited men at Ziegenberg no longer believed that there was a V-3, and neither did Kesselring. "Well, gentlemen," he announced sardonically, "I am the new V-3!"

While the Germans were trying to absorb the shock of Remagen, General Bradley flew to Luxembourg city to talk to General Patton about a new plan he had in mind; the capture of the bridge had opened up opportunities not only at Remagen but elsewhere. When Bradley arrived, Patton was having a shave and a haircut. Hospitably, he sent for a second barber and, under steaming towels in adjoining chairs, the commanders of the Twelfth Army Group and the Third Army discussed the next moves they could make to help hasten Germany's downfall.

As Bradley was well aware, Patton had been fretful over his secondary role in the Rhineland. All through February, the Third Army had been limited to an "aggressive defense," as specified in Eisenhower's overall plan of action for the west bank. Patton had, to be sure, interpreted his orders liberally. His forces had punched through the West Wall fortifications bordering Luxembourg, taken the key communications centers of Prüm and Bitburg and fanned out across the uplands of the western part of the Eifel—all the while netting 1,000 prisoners a day from a steadily weakening German Seventh Army.

But with the formal launching of Bradley's Operation Lumberjack at the end of February, Patton had dropped all pretense of merely probing. On March 1, Third Army elements had moved southward and seized the city of Trier on the Moselle River, capturing one of its bridges intact. On March 5, other forces had jumped the Kyll River and moved eastward toward the Rhine. By March 7, the day of Remagen, the tank crews of Major General Hugh J. Gaffey's crack 4th Armored Division were overlooking the Rhine north of the city of Coblenz. They had made the 55-mile dash from Bitburg in 48 hours—boldly carving a salient through the enemy's lines that was no wider than the road on which they traveled. On March 8, Third Army forces had linked up with elements of the U.S. First Army, tightening the noose around the German troops in the Eifel.

Patton was now impatient to push on, and the plan he discussed with Bradley that day would exercise his restless energies to the fullest. The plan involved a breakout from Bradley's sector of the front to speed progress toward the Rhine in the sector just to the south: the Saar-Palatinate, assigned to the Sixth Army Group under General Devers.

In some ways, Devers' impending drive to close to the Rhine—code-named Operation Undertone and scheduled to start March 15—faced difficulties greater than those in the sectors to the north. The sheer size of the Saar-Palatinate was a problem. Encompassing an area of more than 3,000 square miles, it formed a huge triangle with the Rhine as the base. Reaching the river from some of Undertone's jump-off points would require the attackers to cover as much as 75 miles, a distance greater than those faced at jump-off points anywhere else along the Allied front. The south side of the triangle was guarded by the strongest section of Germany's West Wall defenses, built to face the historic German-French battlegrounds of Alsace and Lorraine.

Despite these difficulties, there were several cogent reasons for an assault on the Saar-Palatinate. This region and the Ruhr were Germany's last great sources of matériel for its war machine. The Germans drew on the Saar basin's coal fields and Lorraine's iron-ore deposits for about 10 per cent of their iron and steelmaking capacity. One of their last functioning synthetic-fuel plants was located at Homburg. Armament factories and chemical works abounded; on the Rhine at Ludwigshafen, a plant owned by the industrial colossus I. G. Farben was manufacturing almost half of Germany's output of chemicals.

Militarily, Devers' forces would be in superb position once they reached the Rhine. Along that 120-mile stretch of the river, and especially between the cities of Mainz and Mannheim, lay some of the Rhine's best natural crossing sites: grassy plains and generally flat terrain that afforded swift access to Germany's interior.

Bradley's plan for helping Undertone would turn Patton loose to exploit the Third Army's freshly won gains. From Trier, at the northern end of the Saar-Palatinate's West Wall, Patton could send his forces sweeping southward to fall upon the fortifications from the rear, while Devers' forces hammered at them in a frontal attack.

Patton was delighted at the prospect. And he was almost

gleeful when Bradley confided another motive for the plan. Field Marshal Montgomery had asked for more of Bradley's troops for his own Rhine crossing later in March. Bradley felt that Monty already had all the men he needed, including the U.S. Ninth Army. Once the Third Army was engaged in the Saar-Palatinate, Bradley would have no spare forces to send Montgomery, for his First Army was already committed to an assault on the Ruhr.

Eisenhower quickly approved Bradley's plan and Devers agreed, though not with much enthusiasm. Devers had planned to have the French First Army, with its 11 divisions, guard the southern flank of Operation *Undertone* while the 14 divisions of the U.S. Seventh Army made the main assault. The Seventh's commander, Lieut. General Alexander M. Patch, had led the army in the invasion of southern France the previous August, and Devers felt that Patch alone could handle the campaign. Patch himself, as self-effacing as Patton was flamboyant, raised no objections to Patton's participation. "We are all in the same army," he said, "and the objective is to destroy the enemy."

The awareness that they were confronting that fate—destruction—hung heavy on the German generals in the Saar-Palatinate. On the day that Operation *Undertone* began, an appeal reached Field Marshal Kesselring from the commander in the area, SS General Paul Hausser of Army Group G, urgently seeking permission to pull the entire German Seventh Army back across the Rhine. Kesselring said no, hold in place. The next day, March 16, Hausser tried again, with the same result.

There were excellent reasons for Hausser's forebodings. Many of his best combat troops were gone, sent to help deal with the Allied penetrations farther north. His two armies were understrength and spread thin. The First Army, which was deployed at the western and southern edges of the Saar-Palatinate along the approaches to the West Wall, had a stretch of 80 miles to defend. At the northern edge of the region, 75 miles of the Moselle River had to be defended; this task fell to Hausser's Seventh Army, already badly battered by Patton's forces in the Eifel and put to flight southward across the Moselle.

The hinge between the two armies lay near Trier, now Patton territory. Since capturing the city on March 1, Pat-

ton's forces had established a 15-mile-deep salient to the south. Hausser rightly assessed this wedge as a potentially catastrophic threat to both of his armies. Both could be trapped from the rear by a multipronged American thrust from the salient. Only one substantial obstacle stood in the Americans' way. Southeast of the salient loomed the Hunsrück Mountains, a region of high, wooded hills, deep ravines and poor roads. In the opinion of the Germans, the terrain was definitely unsuitable for tanks.

Patton thought otherwise. In the early hours of March 13, the 80th and 94th Infantry Divisions of Major General Walton H. Walker's XX Corps moved into the Hunsrück region to open the way for Patton's armor by capturing three critical mountain crossroads towns; the advance proceeded against heavy small-arms and mortar fire from scattered German positions.

Patton himself was so confident of the outcome that during the day he took time to address a letter to General Marshall in Washington about an assignment he wanted after the war in Europe was over. "I should like to be considered for any type of combat command, from a division up, against the Japanese," Patton wrote. "I am sure that my method of fighting would be successful. I also am of such an age that this is my last war, and I would therefore like to see it through to the end."

On March 14, a counterattack by a regiment of the 6th SS Mountain Division, one of General Hausser's most dependable units, slowed the Americans in the Hunsrück. But by the next night one of the targeted mountain towns was in American hands and on the following morning the tanks of the 10th Armored Division were passing through the infantry on the way out of the Hunsrück to the Nahe River, 25 miles to the south.

Another armored division was also headed there. Concurrently with the Hunsrück operation, the 5th and 90th Infantry Divisions of Major General Manton S. Eddy's XII Corps had crossed the lower reaches of the Moselle in assault boats. The 4th Armored Division, summoned from its newly won holdings along the Rhine, crossed the Moselle on bridges quickly built by Eddy's engineers.

The Nahe River, Patton's new objective, was critically important. Running across the width of the Saar-Palatinate, the Nahe would serve to fence off the Germans in the north-

The American plan to destroy the German armies within the Saar-Palatinate triangle called for coordinated attacks from three directions by the U.S. Third and Seventh Armies, with the French First Army in reserve. While the Seventh Army slammed into the West Wall between Saarbrücken and Haguenau, the XX Corps of the Third Army was to drive eastward from Trier and hit the enemy from the rear. In the meantime, from the northern tip of the triangle near Coblenz, the XII Corps was to sweep southward to seal off the German escape.

ern third of the region from those in the south, and lessen the chances of their escape to the Rhine.

Patton had jumped the gun on Operation *Undertone,* surprising neither General Patch nor anyone else who knew his urge to compete.

Patch launched *Undertone,* as scheduled, at 1:00 a.m. on March 15. The 14 divisions of the U.S. Seventh Army, augmented by the Algerian 3rd Infantry Division on loan from the French First Army, moved out of their forward positions in Alsace three corps abreast. The frontal assault on the West Wall was to be made along 40 miles of fortifications from Saarbrücken southeast to Haguenau. The distances to be covered before reaching the wall ranged from as little as

a mile at the northern end of the attack line to as much as 20 miles at the southern end.

The Germans had strengthened the approaches to the wall with antitank ditches, roadblocks and unusually extensive minefields; one that guarded the old fortress town of Bitche contained—according to an engineer's map later captured from the Germans—exactly 3,839 antitank and antipersonnel mines. Narrow paths for the U.S. infantry to use were cleared through the fields by platoons of engineers, working on their knees under intense mortar, artillery and small-arms fire.

Private First Class Silvestre S. Herrera earned a Medal of Honor in a minefield that first day. Herrera, a rifleman with

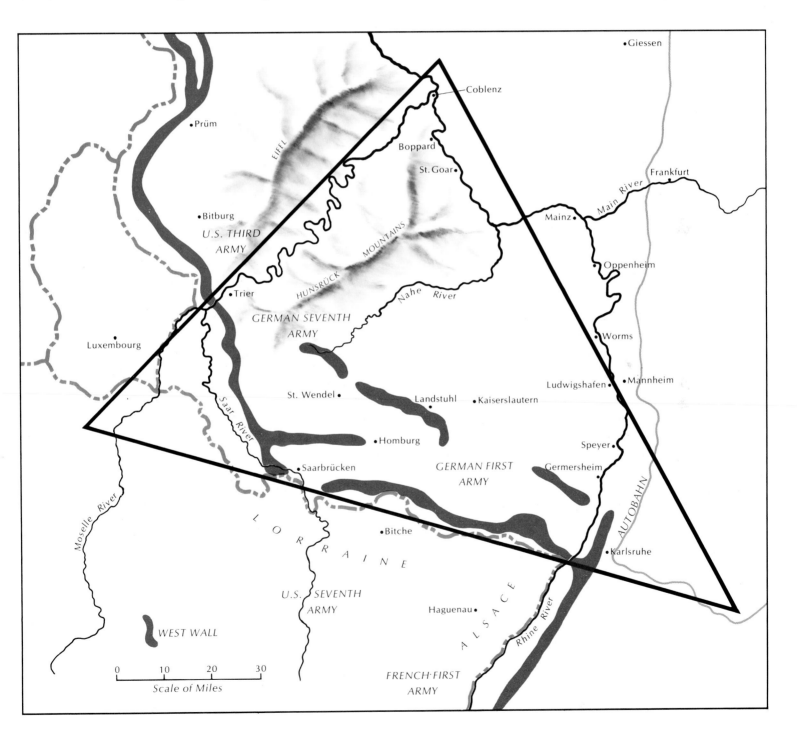

the 36th Infantry Division, had already made a one-man charge against a German strong point, capturing eight prisoners, when his platoon was pinned down by fire from another enemy position across a minefield. Charging again, Herrera stepped on a mine that blew off both his feet. But he could still use his rifle. He kept the Germans under fire until the other men in his platoon took them from the flank.

At the West Wall, Patch's forces found some pillboxes unoccupied; the officers had told their units to pull out and head for the Rhine. In other places, though, German units fought fiercely. Prisoners from these outfits later gave the Americans a clue to their stubbornness. An order by the Führer—which each soldier had been required to sign—had warned that "any man who is captured without being wounded or having fought to the last will be disgraced and his family will be cut off from all government support."

Most of the fortifications proved tough to take. Using techniques learned in U.S. attacks on other sections of the West Wall in the autumn of 1944, infantry and armor would advance under cover of an artillery barrage. Self-propelled

Nearing the Rhine in March 1945, a self-propelled 105mm howitzer with its gun crew riding on its deck roars past an antitank obstacle bearing a menacing slogan scrawled by a German. Such threats amused the Allied troops, who then outnumbered the retreating enemy 3 to 1.

artillery and tanks would fire at the embrasures in the pill-boxes while the engineers, with the help of the infantry, employed high-explosive charges to blow holes in the lines of concrete dragon's teeth designed to entrap tanks. The tanks would move through to the next obstacle, antitank ditches, where they would halt and fire at the pillboxes. After the engineers used bulldozers to fill in the ditches or laid down treadway bridging material, the tanks would cross for a closer encounter—"a slugging match," as one participant put it—with the pillboxes.

These strongholds, containing machine guns and antitank guns, were sometimes 30 feet wide, 50 feet deep and 25 feet high, with at least half the structure underground. Walls and roofs, as much as eight feet thick, were built of concrete and wire mesh and reinforced with steel beams. Access to the pillbox was usually by tunnel from an entrance about 150 yards away. Hand grenades and burning gasoline tossed in through the apertures had little effect. Special explosive charges, detonated on the roof, worked better.

While Patch's forces continued to pound at the West Wall, Patton's tank crews established a bridgehead over the Nahe River. Late on the night of March 16, the 10th Armored Division—using searchlights to help it fight in the dark—broke out, swept southwestward to St. Wendel, only 20 miles from the city of Saarbrücken, and made contact with Patch's troops.

On the morning of the 17th, General Hans Felber, commander of the German Seventh Army, launched a desperate two-division counterattack against the 4th Armored Division's bridgehead on the Nahe. The assault was a farce: One of Felber's divisions was so short of transport that it could not assemble in time to attack; the other division's route to battle was blocked when panic-stricken inhabitants of villages along the way closed their antitank barriers.

That day Army Group G's General Hausser addressed a new appeal to Field Marshal Kesselring for permission to withdraw the German Seventh Army across the Rhine. The order came back to "hold present positions but avoid encirclement and annihilation of the main body of troops." Hausser seized on this ambiguity. He instructed Felber to pull what was left of his army eastward beyond the Nahe in preparation for a retreat to the Rhine's east bank. The defense of the entire Saar-Palatinate triangle fell to the German First Army under its newly designated commander, General Hermann Foertsch.

Foertsch faced the problem of fighting the Americans on two fronts, one of them definable and the other anything but. He could track the movements of Patch's forces, but Patton's forces seemed to be everywhere at once—attacking the West Wall's concrete casements from the rear, racing through the center of the Palatinate, sweeping southward along the Rhine itself.

On March 19 alone, the Third Army overran more than 950 square miles of territory. Coblenz was captured, and two more cities along the Rhine were within reach: Patton's tanks were just 10 miles from Mainz, six miles from Worms.

On March 20, while Patton's armor was churning toward Kaiserslautern, the second-largest city in the Palatinate, three of Patch's divisions penetrated the West Wall. In some places, the German defenses simply collapsed. The 45th Division's advance was so rapid by now that in one captured pillbox a German switchboard was still operating. Two lieutenants who understood German were sent for. Listening, they heard an SS captain issuing orders to his troops to destroy all telephones in the bunkers and prepare to withdraw to the town of Landstuhl. Fighter planes of the American XII Tactical Air Command, the supporting air arm of Operation *Undertone*, had no trouble finding and shattering the target—a three-column convoy of German vehicles that extended for miles.

Both German armies were now on the run. On the night of the 20th, General Felber, his personal staff and other officers of the German Seventh Army began to make their painful way across the Rhine, using ferries, rafts, small boats, anything that floated. And in dense woods south of Kaiserslautern, the men of the German First Army, under relentless attack by U.S. planes, were plodding along the Palatinate's last escape route, hoping to get through to the Rhine and to haven on the east bank.

While Patton and Patch were on the move in the south, Montgomery was still preparing to cross the Rhine in the north. The impetuosity of the Americans was not for him. He saw no need to abandon the basic precept of his long military career: the belief that no battle should ever be launched until after the most meticulous planning. Time, place and method of attack had to be carefully calculated, troops rigorously rehearsed, supplies massed in abundance and within ready reach.

The preparations for Operation *Plunder,* Montgomery's crossing of the Rhine, began well before the end of *Veritable, Grenade* and *Blockbuster*—the preliminary operations designed to gain Allied control of the northernmost area of the Rhineland west of the river. In mid-February, while the savage battle for the Reichswald was still going on, Montgomery had removed elements of the British Second Army to a quiet sector behind the front, along the Maas River, to prepare for *Plunder.* The Maas provided practice in the han-

dling of assault boats. To keep in condition, seasoned troops were sent on grueling runs through the countryside. Newly arrived reinforcements went through battle-indoctrination courses with live ammunition skimming over their heads and the recorded sounds of war dinning in their ears.

The heaviest work load fell to the engineers; some 60,000 of them took part in the preparations, including 22,000 from the U.S. Ninth Army, which was to be the British Second Army's partner in *Plunder.* To expedite the movement of the 1.25 million men and 300,000 tons of matériel that Montgomery intended to have at his disposal at the time of the Rhine jump-off, the engineers built nine bridges across the

U.S. Third Army troops thread their way along a road littered with the wreckage of a retreating German column hit by fighter-bombers near Bad Dürkheim in March of 1945. In some 12,000 sorties flown during a 10-day period of the German withdrawal, American planes destroyed more than 4,000 vehicles and crippled entire German divisions.

Maas, extended rail lines, hacked out new roads and widened others, constructed airfields and bulldozed sites for supply depots and bridge parks—giant parking lots to hold the massive bridging equipment that would be needed to span the Rhine.

The Rhine itself was the object of intensive study. Samplings of the sand-and-gravel riverbed indicated that there would be no problem finding an adequate foundation for bridge pilings. But there were other potential obstacles. Within the *Plunder* zone, each side of the river was bordered by a flood plain, part of the ancient Rhine delta where for eons the river had shifted again and again, creating great loops. To control the course of the river for barge and boat traffic, dikes had been built to cut off or contain the unneeded loops, but they remained as marshes or lakes—a hindrance to cross-country movement.

The dikes themselves were obstacles. Some dikes, built close to the river to contain only the high water of summer, averaged no more than about five feet high and were therefore manageable. But other dikes, built well inland to contain record wintertime floods, were as much as 16 feet high and barred easy access to the river. The engineers' solution was to breach the high dikes with bulldozers or dynamite, then level the breaches into access roads. Once across the river, they would repeat the process to provide exit roads deeper into Germany.

On March 9, Montgomery finally set a firm date for the start of *Plunder*—March 24. As troops and armor began streaming into the assembly areas, the field marshal took steps to conceal the strength and disposition of his attack forces. As a basic precaution, civilians living in and around the *Plunder* zones were sent to the rear; in one Ninth Army sector alone, the Mörs-Homberg district, squads of soldiers evacuated more than 35,000 residents. Elaborate deception measures were also taken. To confound reconnoitering Luftwaffe pilots, dummy guns were fashioned and installed in dummy emplacements, with a few troops assigned to give the positions a lived-in look. Depots were built on sites far from the projected attack areas, filled with dummy vehicles and covered with camouflage netting.

The men of the Ninth Army—perhaps because their commander, General Simpson, matched Montgomery in his passion for tight security—entered into the deception game with gusto. One of their more convoluted schemes centered on the city of Krefeld, which they had taken on March 2 after their breakout from the Roer River. The scheme's purpose was to convince any informers among the remaining inhabitants that the Ninth intended to cross the Rhine nearby. The real crossing site was, in fact, well north of the city.

Working noisily by night with bulldozers and tankdozers, the Ninth's engineers built several access roads to what appeared to be favorable crossing sites in the Krefeld area. Meanwhile, a dummy bridge park was set up in a woods west of the city, and the Krefelders were pointedly ordered to give the place a wide berth. Then, for the benefit of the insatiably curious, the Ninth's deceivers set up a regular routine. In broad daylight a treadway bridge company would roll into the park, ostentatiously unload its equipment—some under trees to indicate an intent to conceal from the air—and depart. At night the company would return, reload and leave, while other trucks would arrive bearing dummy assault boats and pontoons and other spurious supplies to replace the genuine loads. Sure enough, in time the Luftwaffe showed up, as expected, and expended some of its dwindling strength in repeated raids on the park, wiping out large amounts of dummy supplies that had been fabricated in secret in a Krefeld factory.

Perhaps the most sophisticated item in the Allies' bag of tricks was a chemical compound known as "fog oil." Burned in huge generators that were strategically placed parallel to the Rhine, the oil produced a smoke screen 50 or more miles long and up to a mile wide. To the men working inside it, the manufactured fog was little more of a nuisance than a natural fog would have been. But across the river the effect was befuddling. Laid down continuously from dawn to dusk, day after day, the smoke screen shielded the details of Montgomery's build-up from enemy observation points and artillery emplacements on the far side.

For all the subterfuge, the Germans were not fooled. To determine the general scope of the impending assault and the probable crossing sites, they had only to put two and two together. As Field Marshal Kesselring later noted, "The enemy's air operations in a clearly limited area, bombing raids on headquarters, and the smoke screening and assembly of bridging material" gave clues to the Allies' intentions.

Leaving the captured German village of Scheibenhardt, French soldiers use a makeshift bridge to cross a stream on the outskirts of the gutted tow

VENGEFUL VICTORIES BY THE FRENCH

Nearly five years after the German blitz-krieg that conquered their country, French soldiers turned the tables on their bitter enemy and, in March 1945, invaded Germany with the Allies. An urge for revenge spurred on all the disparate elements of the French First Army—soldiers who had followed Charles de Gaulle into exile, underground fighters who had joined the army after liberation, North African troops who had served gallantly in the Allied assaults on Italy and southern France.

On the 19th of March, the French attacked the village of Scheibenhardt just across the border from Alsace-Lorraine. The town soon fell—the Frenchmen's first German prize. "It was," said commandin general Jean de Lattre de Tassigny, ' great day for French hearts."

And others like it lay ahead. By Marc 25, the French had breached the We Wall and reached the Rhine River—at cost of 885 casualties. But in their victor ous sweep into Germany, the troops hac as one French general said, "realized dream held through years of hidden rage.

Astride his horse, a French Moroccan soldier advances carrying live food rations: a goat slung over his saddle. The Goumiers, as they were called, had refused to leave North Africa without their mounts.

Tunisian infantrymen move out from Scheibenhardt, where they had overwhelmed the Germans in hand-to-hand combat.

Still, Kesselring had no illusions about the difficulties of the defense. Since becoming Commander in Chief West, he had cast a fresh eye over his forces and had found them unequal to the task. He later said, "I felt like a concert pianist who is asked to play a Beethoven sonata before a large audience on an ancient, rickety and out-of-tune instrument."

To stand off the 31 divisions that would take part in the Allied onslaught, the Germans had what remained of their once-powerful First Parachute Army: 13 divisions, including seven infantry, four paratroop and, in reserve, the two divisions of the 47th Panzer Corps. Every one of the divisions was understrength; one paratroop division with a normal complement of 16,000 men was now down to about 6,000. All told, the First Parachute Army numbered some 70,000 men. Another 30,000 or so were available from *Volkssturm* (home guard) units in the area, but they could scarcely be counted as a bulwark. And even among the Army regulars, only the elite paratroopers and the tough panzer crews were expected to put up a real fight.

The Germans were also short of matériel—everything from ammunition to armored vehicles. The panzer corps had only 35 tanks—about a quarter of the original complement. As against some 5,500 guns that *Plunder* would deploy, the defenders had approximately 550. To protect the air routes to the industrial Ruhr, strong antiaircraft defenses, including 88mm and 128mm guns that could double as antitank weapons, had long been a fixture in the landscape. But the ground defenses showed signs of the haste with which they had been constructed—mostly in the few weeks since the Germans' retreat from the Rhine's west bank. Built by civilian labor, many of the fortifications were simply earthworks that took little advantage of the terrain. Along the river's east bank, at points where the enemy was believed likely to cross, the defense consisted of a thin line of newly dug rifle and machine-gun pits.

The German commanders were seeing the bitter fruits of their Führer's injunction to hold the west bank at all costs. They had lost the time they needed to strengthen the east bank's defenses and had lost the forces needed to man them. An estimated 38,000 German soldiers had been killed and 51,000 others taken prisoner in the battle for the lower Rhineland's west bank. Those who had made it back to the east bank, and the forces they joined there, were predictably disheartened. Habit and training, rather than morale, would keep them fighting.

Kesselring himself could see no hope on the horizon. On the 19th of March, 10 days after Hitler had personally assured him that help for the Western Front would sooner or later be forthcoming, a new decree from Berlin signaled an ominous shift in the Führer's plans. No mention was made of turning back the enemy tide; instead, the edict took for granted that the tide would roll relentlessly forward. Under the supervision of the local gauleiters, the pliant Nazi officials whom Hitler had always trusted more than his generals, everything that could conceivably be "of immediate or future use to the enemy" was to be destroyed: industrial plants, electrical facilities, waterworks, gasworks, bridges, railway installations, ships, locomotives, freight cars—even food and clothing stores.

It was a measure that could victimize only Hitler's own subjects. "When he saw himself doomed," Minister of Armaments and War Production Albert Speer later wrote, "he consciously desired to annihilate the German people and to destroy the last foundations of their existence." Speer managed to circumvent the edict; he personally persuaded a number of the officials involved to ignore it. But the fact that the edict had been issued at all created great consternation among the generals.

Two Allied actions added substantially to Kesselring's burdens. On March 21, Allied bombers attacking German installations as a prelude to *Plunder's* impending jump-off scored a direct hit on the headquarters of General Schlemm, the First Parachute Army's commander. Schlemm himself—the mastermind of the tenacious defense of the west bank—was so seriously wounded that he had to be replaced. The replacement was General Günther Blumentritt, who had served as Rundstedt's chief of staff in Normandy.

Kesselring was still pondering the loss of Schlemm's services in the north when worse tidings arrived from his commanders in the south. On the night of March 22, a surprise crossing of the Rhine was made by elements of General Patton's Third Army—without benefit of a standing bridge like the one their fellow GIs had used at Remagen, and also without benefit of artillery preparation or aerial bombing.

The crossing site was 10 miles south of the city of Mainz

at the village of Oppenheim, where terraced vineyards grew the grapes for Rhine wine. Oppenheim had seen at least one event that was bound to appeal to Patton's ardent sense of history. Napoleon had crossed the Rhine nearby in eastward pursuit of his foes. But Oppenheim's most interesting feature for Patton was a barge harbor on the west bank, so situated that it could not be seen from across the river. In the dark of the night, six battalions of Patton's 5th Infantry Division, commanded by Major General S. Leroy Irwin, simply piled into assault boats and rafts hidden in the harbor and headed for the opposite shore. To the astonishment of the Americans, the Germans apparently had only one platoon guarding the east bank.

In the morning, while Third Army engineers were building bridges to speed the passage of added infantry and the tanks of the 4th Armored Division, Patton telephoned Bradley at Twelfth Army Group headquarters in Namur. "Brad," he said, lowering his high-pitched voice, "don't tell anyone, but I'm across."

"Well, I'll be damned," said Bradley. "You mean across the Rhine?"

"Sure am. I sneaked a division over last night. But there are so few Krauts around there they don't know it yet. So don't make any announcement—we'll keep it a secret until we see how it goes."

But later that day, after Patton's gunners had knocked down 33 German planes attempting to disrupt his bridge-building efforts, Patton telephoned Bradley again and revoked his plea for secrecy: "Brad, for God's sake, tell the world we're across! I want the world to know that the Third Army made it before Monty starts across!"

Bradley happily obliged with an announcement to the press and radio correspondents at his headquarters. A point was made of the precise hour of Patton's crossing—10:00 p.m. on March 22. Montgomery had advanced the timing of his operation, but as Bradley well knew, it was still not scheduled to begin before 9:00 p.m. on March 23. However, Montgomery was unruffled by the word of Patton's coup.

Late in the afternoon of March 23, after a final favorable report by his weather experts, Montgomery notified his commanders to be ready to go. "Two if by sea" were the code words; puckishly, he borrowed a part of the signal that had

sent Paul Revere galloping through the Yankee countryside in 1775 to warn that the British were coming.

Montgomery had a message for his troops as well, an eve-of-battle custom that he regarded as obligatory. The message, couched in man-to-man terms, began with a reminder of what he had said in his previous message at the start of Operation *Veritable* in February—"that we were going into the final and last round." Now, he noted, "the enemy has in fact been driven into a corner, and he cannot escape." Once across the Rhine, Montgomery promised, "we will crack about in the plains of northern Germany, chasing the enemy from pillar to post."

The message ended with a cheery call to battle: "Over the Rhine, then, let us go. And good hunting to you all on the other side."

As darkness fell on March 23, the entire 22-mile front lighted up simultaneously. The overture to Operation *Plunder* had begun with the orchestrated firing of 3,500 field guns and some 2,000 antitank and antiaircraft guns and rocket projectors.

Plunder's primary east-bank objective was the city of Wesel, which the First Parachute Army's General Schlemm had denied to the Allies earlier in March by blowing its two Rhine bridges. Although it was small, Wesel merited another Allied attempt; as the hub of a road, rail and waterways network, it offered a number of avenues of advance. By fanning out to the east, the attackers would be able to seal off the entire northern edge of the Ruhr and simultaneously strike deeper into Germany.

Under Montgomery's plan, the British Second Army was to cross the Rhine to the north of Wesel, from sites near the towns of Rees and Xanten. The U.S. Ninth Army was to cross to the south of Wesel, from sites near the town of Rheinberg. The British were to capture Wesel while the Americans established a bridgehead against a possible German counterthrust from the Ruhr.

The plan worked with the precision that Montgomery prized. The British jumped off first. At 9:00 p.m., under cover of the bombardment, the amphibious personnel carriers known as buffaloes slid into the Rhine, bearing four battalions of the 51st Highland Division; the leading wave landed on the far bank in less than seven minutes. At 10:00 p.m., the 1st Commando Brigade slipped across the river and by

10:30 was forming up on Wesel's outskirts. At that moment, 200 Royal Air Force Lancasters roared in and dropped 1,100 tons of bombs on the city, only 1,500 yards from the waiting Commandos. By 10:45 the planes were gone and Wesel was a burning ruin.

The U.S. Ninth Army's turn was still to come. While it waited, several ingenious GIs, mindful that the assault boats' outboard motors could be cranky when turned over in the cold hours before dawn, kept them covered with chemical heating pads liberated from the medics. At 2:00 a.m., the 30th Division headed for the east bank three regiments abreast, followed an hour later by two regiments of the 79th Division. By then, to the north, the British Second Army's foothold had been reinforced by the 15th Scottish Division, and all along the west bank thousands more troops were massed and ready to pour across.

But there was none of the usual congestion or confusion. Montgomery, a stickler for tidy operations, had set up groups to control traffic on the bank. The bank controllers directed the assembling of both the men and the assorted storm boats, assault boats, ferries and buffaloes that would take them across. From the moment the troops moved up from the rear marshaling areas to the moment they em-

barked, priorities were strictly enforced and disorder prevented before it began.

At Montgomery's tactical headquarters near Venlo, the field marshal was coping with a problem he would have preferred to avoid: the presence of Winston Churchill. The Prime Minister, an irrepressible warrior at heart, had insisted on being on hand for the big show. Left with no choice, Montgomery had hit upon the idea of having Churchill stay with him at his camp. As he explained in a private note to Field Marshal Sir Alan Brooke, Chief of the Imperial General Staff: "I shall then be able to keep an eye on him and see that he goes only where he will bother no one." Churchill and Brooke, with the Prime Minister's secretary and valet, had flown in from England in time for tea on the 23rd—just about the time Montgomery was signaling his commanders that *Plunder* was a "go."

On the morning of March 24, Montgomery and his illustrious guests motored to a hill overlooking the Rhine near Xanten. The best of the show that Churchill wanted to see was about to begin: the spectacle of a huge aerial train of transports and gliders flying in with airborne troops to reinforce *Plunder's* ground attack.

Shortly before 10:00 a.m., the planes began coming in

from the west, the start of a procession that would continue for three hours and 32 minutes. The sight of a sky filled with aircraft was hardly a novelty to the men on the ground; in the last three days alone, preparatory to *Plunder,* Allied pilots had flown more than 16,000 bombing sorties over German installations in and around the area. But the air armada soaring eastward over the Rhine was of a size and splendor that brought wild cheers from the onlookers.

The armada was, in fact, two air fleets—American and British, combined in a stunning performance of Allied might. Flying from 23 bases in France and southern England, they had converged in the skies near Brussels for the climactic scene that now took place above the riverbanks. First came paratroop transports—American C-46s and C-47s—moving in parallel columns. Then came tug planes—Fortresses, Liberators, Lancasters, Stirlings, Halifaxes—each with two infantry-carrying gliders in tow at the end of long cables. All told, more than 1,600 planes and 1,300 gliders streamed past. High above them, 900 fighters provided a protective umbrella, and another 2,100 fighters screened the area against possible Luftwaffe attack. But most of the 100 or so German fighters that spotted the armada en route wisely avoided engaging.

The Diersfordterwald, a stretch of high, wooded ground a few miles north of Wesel, was the armada's objective. As it came into view, the transports descended to as low as 350 feet to disgorge the paratroopers, and the gliders sailed to earth with their infantry loads. More than 21,000 troops were delivered by air to the battlefront—two entire divisions, the British 6th Airborne and the U.S. 17th Airborne.

Montgomery's schedule called for a linkup of airborne and ground troops before the day was done. The goal was met, though not without cost. Many of the transports returning from the mission, doors open and parachute strings hanging, were crippled and in flames; one observer counted 23 burning aircraft at one time. For other planes there was no journey back.

The airborne troops, now earthbound infantrymen, encountered varying resistance. Some of the defenders scattered or quickly surrendered—as one gun crew did when a glider set down smack on top of the gun pit. Other Germans fought on with mortars and machine guns and sniper fire.

Some paratroopers used knives and rifle butts to subdue resisters, and in one instance matters were settled in a truly bizarre fashion. A company of the Canadian 1st Parachute Battalion was holding a village that was under heavy shelling by the Germans' 88s when a Luftwaffe pilot, one of the few to fly that day, landed his plane between the two positions. "Both sides wanted him," recalled Private J. A. Collins. "He did not know where to go. Three of our fellows ran out and made him prisoner. During the first stages of capture he was very cocky. One of our sergeants challenged him to a fist fight, and the German pilot took him on. He gave an excellent account of himself, but the sergeant knocked him down at last and he did not wish to continue."

By early afternoon the Germans' resistance was crumbling. Swarming through one command post, troops of the U.S. 194th Combat Team captured the colonel in charge and were leading him out when his orderly rushed over with an armful of papers. "Sir," he called, "you forgot your maps!" One of the Americans seized them; they revealed the location of every German installation and troop disposition in the surrounding area.

By nightfall on March 24, the airborne mission had achieved its first-day aims and more. The high ground of the Diersfordterwald was secured. Six miles east of the Rhine, British and American troops were at the Issel, the next river to be crossed in the Allied sweep forward; five of the Issel's bridges had been taken intact and held against German tank counterattacks. And back at the Rhine, elements of the U.S. 17th Airborne Division had made contact with the British Commandos in Wesel.

Though the last German holdouts were still to be dislodged, the work of clearing the city was well under way. Mountains of rubble, the bequest of the RAF bombing the night before, had to be removed with dispatch: U.S. Ninth Army engineers were slated to put three bridges across the Rhine at Wesel the next day. The arduous task of unclogging Wesel's waterfront and streets fell to the black troops of the 1698th U.S. Engineer Combat Battalion. Moving in only hours after the Commandos had entered the city, they put their bulldozers to added use—helping the Commandos reduce the remaining German strong points.

South of Wesel, the Ninth Army had found the initial going comparatively easy, swiftly overrunning the Germans'

Prime Minister Winston Churchill, accompanied by Britain's Field Marshal Sir Bernard L. Montgomery (second from rear), rides nonchalantly across the Rhine in an amphibious buffalo on March 25, 1945. According to an officer who was in the party, the Prime Minister "seemed more perturbed about lighting his cigar in the wind than about shellfire."

UNLEASHING THE THUNDERBOLTS AND TYPHOONS

By the spring of 1945, Hermann Göring's once-vaunted Luftwaffe was not able to maintain an effective defense anywhere over Germany. The bombers and fighter-bombers of the Allied tactical air forces—several thousand planes—ranged at will over the battlefields and rear areas. So terrible was the destruction that German Field Marshal Walther Model offered a 10-day furlough to any soldier "who knocks down a strafer with his infantry weapon."

With fewer enemy aircraft to engage, such fighters as the British Hawker Tempest and Typhoon and the U.S. P-47 Thunderbolt were pressed into ground-attack roles, carrying rockets and 1,000-pound bombs to augment their machine guns and 20mm cannon. Sweeping along on low-level missions of opportunity, they blasted everything in sight: railroads, bridges and viaducts, airfields and munitions depots and retreating German columns.

Front-line air support became a highly polished art. Forward air controllers traveled with the Allied troops, and called in the planes by radio whenever the enemy was encountered. To speed their reaction time, the fighter-bomber units often maintained a constant protective umbrella over the spearheads.

Fighter pilots sometimes groused about these air-to-ground missions; no one became an ace by shooting up tanks. But the tactical air forces were vital to winning the War: In one two-week span, the U.S. Ninth Air Force destroyed or damaged no fewer than 896 enemy tanks and armored vehicles, 10,220 trucks, 969 locomotives, 19,019 rail cars and 2,634 buildings. Eisenhower later commented on "the extraordinary influence of the airplanes during our speedy dashes across Germany. Without it those pursuits could never have accomplished such remarkable results."

A ground crewman loads rockets under the wing of a P-47 Thunderbolt. Though the rockets carried only relatively small explosive charges, their penetrating power made them ideal against such targets as tanks.

British Typhoons use rockets to soften up a cluster of fortified houses in the town of Kalkar in northern Germany in advance of a ground assault. Later the Wiltshire Regiment was able to enter the town unopposed.

Laden with two 1,000-pound bombs, a Typhoon splashes up a rain-sodden runway in Holland. Its target was a north German rail line being used to reinforce units opposing Montgomery's advance to the Rhine.

In this view from an orbiting American plane, engineers assemble a bridge across the Rhine south of Mainz. The aircraft is a light "puddle jumper" used by spotters to call in air support in case of enemy action.

forward lines and pushing inland as far as six miles. On the left flank, the 30th Division had reached the Lippe River, the line of demarcation between its troops and those of the British Second Army. On the right, the 79th Division had taken the major town of Dinslaken and was pointing southeastward toward the fringes of the Ruhr. And in the Ninth's crossing area, the first of *Plunder's* Rhine bridges had been completed—a 1,150-foot treadway that the engineers had put up in the record time of nine hours.

The worst of the fighting on *Plunder's* first day—and for several days and nights thereafter—befell the 51st Highland Division, on the extreme left flank of the British Second Army. Assigned to the northernmost crossing site at Rees, the men of the 51st ran into deep trouble immediately upon reaching the far shore.

Confronting the Highlanders were the best German forces anywhere in the *Plunder* area: the veteran paratroopers of the 2nd Parachute Corps, with the equally seasoned 47th Panzer Corps behind them in reserve. The arsenal of the parachute corps was badly depleted; the commander, General Eugen Meindl, later estimated that he had no more than 80 field and medium guns, 12 assault guns and 60 of the 88mm dual-purpose guns. But his paratroopers were deployed in the unbroken units of a traditional field army, and they fought—as their adversaries put it—"like madmen."

Rees was defended by a single battalion of paratroopers. They soon made it abundantly clear that the town would have to be taken from them street by street, house by house. Early in the fighting, the Highlanders' commander, Major General Thomas G. Rennie, was killed by a mortar shell. A decision was made to detail some of the Highlanders to bypass Rees and go on to seize the village of Speldrop, a mile and a half inland.

The Black Watch battalion assigned to the mission tried three times. Each time it was routed in savage counterattacks by paratroop infantry aided by tanks, 88s and self-propelled guns. In the retreat, two Black Watch companies were left behind, cut off. Troops of the Highland Light Infantry of Canada, the first Canadians to cross the Rhine, were dispatched for another try. As they prepared to set out, Private Malcolm B. Buchanan asked a Black Watch soldier who had returned from Speldrop about his comrades still in the village. "All dead or captured," he said. "Shoot anything that moves because it will be a Jerry."

Preceded by a rolling barrage from the British guns on the Rhine's west bank, the Canadians crossed at intervals over the 800 yards of open field that led into Speldrop. Sheets of enemy machine-gun, mortar and artillery fire greeted them. "I don't believe they like us here," a lieutenant in a Bren carrier said wryly to his driver. A few minutes later he was dead, blown into the air by a shellburst.

In the town, Private Buchanan kicked open the door of the first house he reached, ignored several dead German soldiers in the kitchen and prepared to toss a grenade down the cellar steps. "Don't shoot, for God's sake!" came a voice from below. "Black Watch here!" One by one, the beleaguered men emerged. They had stood off the Germans for hours, using bayonets and shovels and hurling back the enemy's grenades after their own ammunition ran out.

The battle raged through the night, with most of Speldrop in flames and neither side giving any quarter. "Not many prisoners were taken," Private Buchanan recalled. "If they did not surrender before we started on a house, they never had the opportunity afterward." In the morning, signs of a German weakening appeared. A Canadian patrol sent out beyond the village had no trouble whatever bagging several enemy machine-gun crews: They were fast asleep at their posts, as exhausted as the Canadians were.

Speldrop was secured by noon. The men of the Highland Light Infantry were replaced and sent to a rest area. Late that night they began to wonder if the nickname they had given themselves—"Hell's Last Issue," for the brigade's initials—was perhaps a bit too apt. They were needed for another aid mission. Five miles from Speldrop, the North Nova Scotias and the Argyll and Sutherland Highlanders were having trouble in the town of Bienen, encountering a new level of German desperation: suicidal charges by individual paratroopers. Before midnight on the 25th, the Canadians were on the move again, headed for their second bloody battle in two days. Bienen was secured on the afternoon of the 26th.

By March 28, *Plunder's* forces had expanded their eastbank foothold into a solid bridgehead 35 miles wide and up to 20 miles deep, and 12 new bridges spanned the Rhine to speed the arrival of more divisions and armor. The pace of the operation had exceeded Montgomery's expectations; he had figured it would take two weeks. The opportunity for a breakout into the north German plain, the next item on his agenda, was now clearly within grasp. In a message to his commanders on the 28th, Montgomery formally wrote finis to *Plunder* in one terse sentence: "We have won the Battle of the Rhine."

With this announcement came a listing of new objectives. The British Second and the U.S. Ninth Armies were to advance to the line of the Elbe River, 250 miles east of the Rhine. The Canadian First Army, which had crossed the Rhine after the other two armies, was to turn north to attend to some critical unfinished business in Holland: A bypassed German army, the Twenty-fifth, had to be dealt with.

As it happened, events elsewhere along the Allied front had conspired to put Montgomery in the shade. *Plunder* had been a masterly example of the meticulously planned set-piece attack. The American generals might be as careful in their preparations, but they were improvisers, more aggressive in exploiting every opportunity and in pushing their offensives to the utmost. In large part because of their gains, General Eisenhower now shifted the main thrust of the Allied drive deeper into Germany from Montgomery in the north to Bradley in the center.

Eisenhower had been pondering this change in plan since mid-March, when it became apparent that the initial phase of the battle for Germany would soon be over. Eisenhower had to resolve the question of how best to deploy the Allied forces as they moved farther into Germany for the final assault and a linkup with the Russian armies moving in from the east. And his considerations led him to a conclusion that infuriated his British associates, bewildered some of his own compatriots and delighted the Russians. Eisenhower decided to leave the capture of Germany's capital, Berlin, to the Russians, and to focus the main effort of his forces in central and southern Germany.

Eisenhower knew full well that Roosevelt, Churchill and Stalin had agreed in February at the Yalta Conference that Berlin was to be in the Soviet zone of occupation after the War. But they had made no decision as to the actual capture of Berlin. Nothing prevented Eisenhower from making that decision, and he made it based largely on two premises. One was that by now the Russians were so close to Berlin

that it would be a waste of Allied manpower to move against the city. The other was that a much more useful Allied effort could be directed against a reported German stronghold hundreds of miles to the south—a vast natural refuge in which Hitler and his most dedicated troops supposedly planned to fight on indefinitely.

No one in the Allied camp disputed the need to deal with such a stronghold—if, indeed, it existed. Belief in the possibility was reflected on intelligence maps at Allied headquarters. A giant goose egg was drawn around some 20,000 square miles of mountainous country south of Munich, encompassing the Alpine region of Germany's southernmost province, Bavaria, as well as western Austria and northern Italy. The mapmakers had even come up with a label for the area—Reported National Redoubt.

Information pointing to plans for the redoubt had been coming in since September of 1944, some from cooperative Germans—who called it *Die Alpenfestung* (the Alpine fortress)—and some from Allied secret agents in the area. In February of 1945 the War Department in Washington had issued an advisory urging that field commanders down to corps level be alerted to the possibility. Then, on the eve of Eisenhower's decision, had come what seemed to be the clincher—information that not only took the redoubt's existence for granted but also provided details.

From the U.S. Seventh Army in the south, the intelligence chief reported that enemy supplies had been arriving in the redoubt area since the start of February, brought in on "three to five very long trains" per week; that "a new type of gun" had been observed on many of the trains, and that the construction of an underground aircraft factory "capable of producing Messerschmitts" was said to be under way. The report also mentioned the possibility of the creation in the redoubt of "an elite force, predominantly SS and mountain troops, of between 200,000 and 300,000 men."

The officers around Eisenhower treated the matter with the utmost seriousness. His chief of staff, Lieut. General Walter Bedell Smith, said later: "There was every reason to believe that the Nazis intended to make their last stand among the crags." After repeated analysis of the information at hand, the staff conceded that the Germans might have planted evidence of a redoubt but generally agreed that it was imprudent to dismiss such a stronghold as a hoax.

Ninth Army engineers tug on a rope to release the anchor of an antifrogman barrier before hauling it across the Rhine by launch.

Crewmen moor a hydrogen-filled barrage balloon near a Rhine bridgehead site. General Eisenhower expressly called for the use of the balloons, which had provided antiaircraft protection during the Normandy invasion.

PROTECTING THE VITAL CROSSINGS

With almost 100 Allied bridges of every sort spanning the Rhine by late March, it was obvious that the Germans could muster only nuisance raids against the crossings. But the British and American engineers were nevertheless determined that none of their hard work would be undone.

Elaborate measures were taken for contingencies. The engineers bulldozed gun emplacements at the bridge approaches and dug in batteries of antitank guns. Upstream of most bridges, the engineers installed three barriers: a wire-cable boom capable of halting a vessel as large as a barge, a log boom to detonate floating mines, and a net to entangle one-man submarines or frogmen. Would-be saboteurs were further discouraged by night patrols, which periodically detonated TNT charges in the water.

To balk any remaining Luftwaffe ambitions, the engineers emplaced 90mm antiaircraft cannon and multiple .50-caliber machine-gun mounts around the bridgeheads. And above the roadways flew clusters of barrage balloons, from which were suspended numerous steel cables to protect against low-flying planes.

To the extent that it could, the Luftwaffe mounted angry attacks against the bridges; the Germans flew 200 sorties in the Third Army zone alone. But the engineers could proudly report that not a single bridge anywhere was knocked out by enemy action.

Two U.S. antiaircraft gunners scan the skie

In any case, Eisenhower's conclusion that Berlin should be given over to the Russians was a radical and unexpected change. "On to Berlin!" had been a rallying cry of the Allied forces ever since they landed in Normandy. Eisenhower himself had expected to take Berlin and had said so in a letter to Field Marshal Montgomery on the 15th of September, 1944, describing Berlin as "clearly, the main prize" and adding: "There is no doubt whatsoever, in my mind, that we should concentrate all our energies and resources on a rapid thrust to Berlin."

But a recent turn of events had helped to change Eisenhower's mind. During the Allied drive to the Rhine in late February and early March, with some U.S. units making spectacular gains of up to 35 miles a day, it had seemed entirely possible that Berlin could be within Allied grasp before long; at the time, though the Russians had already reached the Oder River west of the German-Polish border—at a point only about 40 miles east of Berlin—they appeared to have come to a full stop there. But on March 11, Eisenhower's intelligence people had reported a significant Soviet advance: Marshal Georgy K. Zhukov's spearheads had crossed the Oder into Germany and were at Seelow, just 28 miles from Berlin. Eisenhower saw no chance of reaching Berlin first; his own forces that day were still 300 miles away.

What he did not know was that the Seelow report was a red herring. As it turned out, the Russians did not get there until more than a month later. Soviet defense officials admitted as much—long after the War had ended.

The fact was that at Supreme Allied Command headquarters virtually nothing was known of the Red Army's plans or intentions. There was no day-to-day military coordination between east and west field commanders. Most of what Eisenhower and his staff learned about Russian moves came from the Soviet communiqué broadcast nightly by the BBC.

The problem was all the more worrisome because a lack of coordination could spell trouble for both sides as the gap between them narrowed. In 1939, when Stalin and Hitler were allies, German troops advancing into Poland had clashed briefly with Red Army forces racing west. A similar accident on a much larger scale was possible if the Anglo-American forces and the Russians met by surprise.

The prospect was worrying Washington as well. On Eisenhower's desk was a message from General Marshall pointedly reminding him of the dangers, though expressed in the Army Chief of Staff's usual low-key way. "What are your ideas on control and coordination to prevent unfortunate instances?" Marshall had asked. "Steps should now be initiated without delay for communication and liaison."

On March 19, Eisenhower went off for a few days' vacation near Cannes on the French Riviera. The respite gave him an opportunity to mull over the next moves. With Eisenhower, at his invitation, was General Bradley. Always respected and trusted by Eisenhower, Bradley had delighted the Supreme Allied Commander with the smashing successes of his First and Third Armies in recent weeks. Eisenhower was particularly interested to hear Bradley's view of the idea of leaving Berlin to the Russians, and Bradley was as usual forthright.

He began by pointing out that even assuming Field Marshal Montgomery's success in crossing the Rhine—Operation *Plunder* was then just four days off—the rest of the way to Berlin was far from obstacle-free. Another major river, the Elbe, would have to be crossed; moreover, between the Elbe and Berlin lay some 50 miles of lowlands—an area studded with lakes, interlaced with streams and further cut by occasional canals. The terrain itself could slow Montgomery's advance, and the German defenders were unlikely to help speed it up.

Eisenhower asked Bradley for his estimate of the potential cost to the Allies of taking Berlin. About 100,000 casualties, Bradley guessed. That, he added, was "a pretty stiff price to pay for a prestige objective, especially when we've got to fall back and let the other fellow take over." Bradley's opinion helped Eisenhower make up his mind.

On March 28, back at his headquarters at Rheims, Eisenhower set down his decision in a message to Stalin. Though such a direct communication with the Soviet dictator was unprecedented, Stalin was also Commander in Chief of the Soviet armed forces, and the Combined Chiefs had authorized Eisenhower to deal directly with the Soviet High Command on "matters exclusively military in character." He saw no particular reason to consult beforehand with the Combined Chiefs of Staff or with the U.S. or British governments. Not even Eisenhower's Deputy Supreme Commander, British Air Chief Marshal Sir Arthur Tedder, knew in advance about the message to Stalin. Eisenhower merely sent copies to the people involved.

The message detailed Eisenhower's plans. "My immediate operations," it began, "are designed to encircle and destroy the enemy forces defending the Ruhr. My next task will be to divide the remaining enemy forces by joining hands with your forces." The best way to effect this junction, Eisenhower continued, would be for his forces to make their "main effort" in central Germany, along the axis formed by Erfurt, Leipzig and Dresden. Then, when the situation allowed, a secondary advance would be made farther south in the Regensburg-Linz area for an added linkup with Russian forces there, thus "preventing the consolidation of German resistance in Redoubt in southern Germany."

Eisenhower concluded: "Before deciding firmly on my plans, it is, I think, most important they should be coordinated as closely as possible with yours both as to direction and timing. Could you, therefore, tell me your intentions and let me know how far the proposals outlined in this message conform to your probable action. If we are to complete the destruction of German armies without delay, I regard it as essential that we coordinate our action and make every effort to perfect the liaison between our advancing forces. I am prepared to send officers to you for this purpose."

The message was encoded and forwarded to the Anglo-American Military Mission in Moscow, with covering instructions to get it to Stalin and to do everything that could be done to elicit a full reply. A few hours later Eisenhower dispatched two other messages, one to General Marshall in Washington and the other to Field Marshal Montgomery.

For Marshall, Eisenhower had an explanation of why he had selected the Erfurt-Leipzig-Dresden area as the focus of his main effort. It not only offered "the shortest route to present Russian positions" but also would mean overrunning a major industrial area still in German hands. Both the German High Command headquarters and the Reich's government ministries, Eisenhower noted, were said to be evacuating Berlin and moving into the Leipzig-Dresden area.

On the subject of coordination with the Russians, Eisenhower expressed doubt about an earlier Marshall proposal that a demarcation line be fixed between the Allied and Soviet forces. Such a line, he said, would "tie ourselves down." But he proposed to suggest to the Russians that "when our forces meet, either side will withdraw to its own occupational zone at the request of the opposite side."

Eisenhower's message to Montgomery came as a total shock. Just the day before, without consulting Eisenhower, Montgomery had marked his crossing of the Rhine by issuing orders to his field commanders "for the operations eastward," leaving no doubt that his ultimate objective was Berlin. Now, clearly, his mission was to be limited. Eisenhower's message to him not only described Bradley's drive across central Germany as the "main thrust," but also informed Montgomery that once the Ruhr was enveloped he would have to relinquish the services of the U.S. Ninth Army to Bradley. As to what would happen beyond the Elbe, Eisenhower was silent. There was not even a passing reference to Berlin.

In fact, no mention of Berlin appeared in any of the three Eisenhower messages of March 28—and Stalin was quick to grasp the significance of the omission.

Although Russian responses to Allied communications sometimes took weeks, Stalin's reply to Eisenhower arrived on April 1—within 24 hours after Eisenhower's message had reached the Soviet dictator. Stalin was all affability in his response. Eisenhower's plan for dividing the Germans by joining his forces with the Russian forces, Stalin noted, "coincides entirely with the plan of the Soviet High Command." He also agreed that the linkup should take place in the Erfurt-Leipzig-Dresden area, since the Soviet High Command felt that the "main blow" of the Russians "should be delivered in that direction."

Then, as a casual aside, Stalin injected a mention of Berlin—and dismissed it in two sentences. "Berlin has lost its former strategic importance," he declared. "In the Soviet High Command plans, secondary forces will therefore be allotted in the direction of Berlin." Only later were the Allies to learn that at the time of Stalin's message, the Red Army was carrying out a major shift of forces aimed at Berlin as a primary objective.

Eisenhower's cable to Stalin stunned and outraged his British colleagues. Montgomery sent a wire to Field Marshal Brooke: "I consider we are about to make a terrible mistake." The Chief of the Imperial General Staff felt that Eisenhower's performance was inexcusable. "To start with," Brooke answered, "he has no business to address Stalin direct, his communications should be through the Combined Chiefs of Staff; secondly, he produced a telegram which was unintelligible; and finally, what was implied in it appeared to be entirely adrift and a change from all that had been previously agreed on."

In hopes of undoing what they regarded as critical damage to the Allied cause, the British chiefs proposed to General Marshall, representing the American chiefs, that Eisenhower's message to Stalin be recalled until the Combined Chiefs could discuss the matter of Berlin. The response was negative. The American chiefs felt that the war in Germany was clearly at a point where the question of objectives was best answered by the commander on the ground.

Churchill now took a hand by personally appealing to both Eisenhower and Roosevelt to reconsider the Berlin issue. The prospect of Stalin's entrenchment in postwar Europe was never far from Churchill's thoughts. As he wrote to Eisenhower: "I deem it highly important that we should shake hands with the Russians as far east as possible."

A strained and weary Roosevelt—he had less than a month to live—declined to intervene. On April 5 a message from Churchill to the President signaled an end to the British protest. It concluded with a Latin quotation—*Amantium irae amoris integratio est,* "Lovers' quarrels are a part of love"—which the War Department sent on to Eisenhower as a sign of restored Anglo-American amity.

Eisenhower himself remained unmoved throughout the entire flap. So far as he was concerned, Berlin had become "nothing but a geographical location." And in a war, as he later said, "geographical objectives are not the proper objectives. The enemy is. That is what you go after."

A LAST GREAT AIRDROP

Amid the debris of an earlier paratroop drop, glidermen unload their craft and prepare to move out after a massive airborne assault across the Rhine.

ONE MAN'S VIEW OF THE "PARATROOP BUSINESS"

As he followed the American armies from North Africa to Italy and Normandy, *Life's* famed combat photographer Robert Capa had seen, he said, "too many D-days," but he could not resist the opportunity to cover one more: Operation *Varsity*, the airborne assault planned to help Allied ground troops establish a bridgehead across the Rhine around the town of Wesel.

As it turned out, *Varsity* was the last and biggest one-day airborne operation of the War; the enormous forces involved included 3,044 transport planes and gliders, more than 3,000 fighter planes and 21,680 troops of the U.S. 17th and British 6th Airborne Divisions. Capa saw only a fraction of the operation, but his stark pictures, most of them shot in a single hour, captured in unsurpassed detail the paratroopers' tense preparations and fearfully dangerous work.

Early on the morning of March 24, Capa took off from an airfield in France with the 507th Parachute Infantry Regiment of the 17th Airborne. "We dropped down to 600 feet at 10:25, four miles north of the Rhine. Our plane was a hell of a lot hit before we got out of it." Other planes were destroyed, but most held together long enough to release their towed gliders or let their paratroopers jump—"black dots," wrote Capa, "transforming into silken flowers."

At 10:30 a.m. Capa made his own jump safely and began taking pictures. "Some of the men who had jumped after me landed in trees. A German machine gun opened up at the dangling men and they were murdered." But Capa's friends silenced the machine gun, and set up their artillery along the road assigned as their target. They held that road in scattered skirmishes. "At 11:30," Capa said, "we were firmly established. In the afternoon we made our juncture with the other regiments. I closed my camera."

All the units, British and American alike, had done just as well. By 2:00 p.m. they had taken every objective and linked up with the ground troops a few miles south at Wesel. But the victory had been costly for the Allies: more than 500 men killed and 1,250 wounded. Concluded Capa grimly: "There is no future in this paratroop business."

Laden with cameras, photographer Robert Capa crouches on a makeshift steel airstrip just before parachuting across the Rhine with U.S. forces.

A U.S. ''airdough,'' as paratroopers called themselves, stands suited up and ready to go. The circular object on his chest is a quick release for his harness.

Two American paratroopers sit reading on boxcar bumpers at a siding somewhere in France. As part of an elaborate deception, the troopers were shuttled around the country in freight trains before finally winding up at their assigned takeoff points. "After two days of this hocus-pocus," Capa wrote, "we arrived at a camp next to an airfield 60 miles from the spot from which we started."

Resting his foot on bundles of equipment that will accompany him to Germany, a trooper secures a trench knife to his pants leg. The men's personal weaponry included bazookas, automatic rifles and machine guns.

Getting into proper fighting spirit for the jump, U.S. paratroopers of the
507th Regiment shave their heads to leave only an Indian-style scalp lock.
There were other comradely rituals: All the paratroopers on Capa's
plane leaped out the open door yelling not the traditional ''Geronimo!''
but ''Umbriago!'' —a corruption of the Italian word for ''drunk.''

Laden with gear, men of the 17th Airborne clamber aboard a C-46 set to lift them into German rear areas. Each trooper had two parachutes, a main and a reserve, and toted up to 80 pounds of combat gear and supplies.

A team of soldiers wrestles a howitzer into a glider through its hinged front section. More than 100 artillery pieces, along with 109 tons of ammunition, and 695 vehicles made the flight with the troops. Following them by about one hour were 240 B-24 Liberators with another 582 tons of air-dropped supplies.

The German sky is filled with drifting—
and vulnerable—paratroopers. "The moments
between your jump and landing," Capa
said, "are 24 hours in any man's life."

A British Horsa with 30 men skids to a halt in a tilled field. According to Capa, gliders made such good targets on landing that "if the Germans could have put in 20 tanks they could have murdered the gliders."

Cut free from their towplanes, two American Waco gliders swoop toward their assigned landing zones. The battle was already raging below, as evidenced by the farmhouse set ablaze during a skirmish.

*Under enemy fire, a U.S. gliderman risks a
quick getaway on a stray horse. A buddy takes
refuge in the shadow of a grounded glider.*

Carrying his rifle, an American trooper sprints toward a slit trench, taking advantage of the cover provided by a German hedgerow.

A soldier crouches low in a muddy stream, sheltering himself from German fire. With one hand he clutches his carbine; with the other he grasps a slender tree trunk for balance.

A burning German armored half-track, knocked
out by American bazooka fire, straddles a
quiet country lane. The U.S. troopers' bazookas
were also used to destroy 13 German tanks.

A camouflaged German 88mm gun is guarded
by one of the Americans who seized it. To
put these guns out of commission, the troopers
usually spiked them with thermite grenades.

Hands clasped behind their heads, two Germans march ahead
of their captors. In the daylong Operation Varsity, troops of the U.S. 17th
Airborne Division took 2,000 German prisoners, and men of the
British 6th Airborne Division captured another 1,500 of the enemy.

Two young children and their mother, routed from their home during the fighting, find temporary shelter in a foxhole left by the paratroopers. A brand-new pair of boots is the only possession they had time to bring along. In the background another civilian stretches out in the sunlight.

Passing beneath a parachute snared in utility lines, a U.S. paratrooper carries a wounded buddy down a country road to an aid station. Though the 17th Airborne suffered close to 700 casualties that day, the British 6th Airborne was even harder hit, with almost 1,100 killed and wounded.

Heading toward a rendezvous with British ground forces, American paratroopers file past a glider that smashed into a hedgerow on landing. Of the 1,348 gliders that were involved in Operation Varsity, more than 50 per cent were either damaged or completely destroyed.

HURDLING THE FINAL BARRIER

iding amphibious buffaloes, British Second Army troops churn across the Rhine toward landing sites on the eastern shore near Wesel, north of the Ruhr.

A SOLDIER'S DREAM COME TRUE

The mighty river Rhine, the last great barrier protecting Germany in the west, had long been a grave concern for Allied planners. But by the time six American, British and Canadian armies finally drew up on the Rhine's western bank in March 1945, hurdling the major stumbling block had become little more than a field exercise against a shattered enemy who, as one German general admitted, "could only pretend to resist."

In the center, the U.S. First Army had captured a bridge at Remagen and had sent large numbers of troops across the river. In the north, the main thrust was made against Wesel by the British Second and the U.S. Ninth Armies, both of them under Field Marshal Sir Bernard L. Montgomery. Monty's assault—as usual, huge and meticulously prepared—unfolded like clockwork on the night of March 23. Under cover of a ponderous aerial and artillery bombardment, troops sped in motorized craft toward either side of Wesel. As soon as the men were ashore the supply build-up began, and by midmorning craft of every shape and size—including a special detachment of U.S. Navy LCVPs and LCMs—were ferrying men and equipment across the river. In less than three days, the two armies had linked up and engineers had installed 12 floating bridges. Casualties were light for both the British and the Americans.

Meanwhile, far to the south, 80 miles beyond Remagen, Lieut. General George S. Patton of the U.S. Third Army had received orders to "take the Rhine on the run." That noted exponent of the headlong attack disdained to bother with artillery preparation. Immediately, he flung troops of the 5th Division into the river at Oppenheim, and the first company made it across without so much as firing a shot. Patton's quick success paved the way for easy crossings by the U.S. Seventh Army units 20 miles still farther south.

By March 28, Allied troops were pouring across the Rhine into six major bridgeheads along a 200-mile front. All of the assaults, whatever the style of the commanding officer, had proved to be a soldier's dream come true—that rare military venture where everything worked.

British artillery fires across the Rhine in the 3,300-gun bombardment that preceded the crossing of Montgomery's Twenty-first Army Group.

Trucks, troops and assault boats of the U.S. Third Army's 89th Division clog a narrow street in St. Goar prior to an assault crossing on March 26, 1945.

SILENT PADDLERS IN ASSAULT BOATS

At 10 o'clock on the night of March 22, troops of the U.S. Third Army's 5th Division slipped into the Rhine at Oppenheim and, in 500 seven-man assault boats, paddled silently through the cold waters to the eastern shore, some 300 yards distant.

Racing up the firm, sandy bank, they took the defenders completely by surprise. The first group of Germans made haste to throw down their arms. They even volunteered to paddle themselves over to the west bank and surrender to the rest of the men who were still waiting to cross.

The Americans quickly cleared all enemy troops from the bridgehead, and then fanned out into the surrounding area. In the meantime, a contingent of U.S. Navy sailors began speeding infantry reinforcements across the river in LCVPs. An officer summed up the situation as it had applied to all the American units: "There was no real fight to it."

Flying the Stars and Stripes, two U.S. Navy men ferry reinforcements to a secured landing zone.

Chugging across the Rhine in a double assault boat, GIs hunker down to avoid small-arms fire from Germans on the east bank.

Troops of the U.S. Third Army paddle assault boats across the Rhine at St. Goar. In the background a smoke screen settles over the town and riverbank.

Combat engineers of the U.S. Third Army prepare to transport an M-10 tank destroyer and a trailer to a bridgehead on the east bank of the Rhine south of Main

Motorboats push a Bailey-bridge section and a tank destroyer against the swift river current.

ig cargo rafts like this one were put together by laying heavy planking across a string of steel pontoons.

POURING ACROSS MEN AND MATÉRIEL

Once the assault troops of the U.S. Third Army had established bridgeheads on the east bank of the river, combat engineers rushed across tanks, tank destroyers and construction equipment, sometimes using ferries built from floating bridge sections and pushed by motorboats. To the south at Worms, U.S. Seventh Army engineers rafted across more than 1,000 vehicles, including 50 tanks, in 24 hours.

Where currents proved too swift for the small boats, the larger Navy craft took over. The LCMs and LCVPs were ideal cargo ferries, and the LCVPs also could be used to hold in place floating bridge sections during construction. "As soon as they were in the water," an engineer reported, "the entire picture changed."

The big boats made round trips in little more than 15 minutes, even at sites where the distance between loading and landing points was nearly a mile. Indeed, six LCVPs and six LCMs operating in the Third Army's sector managed to ferry across almost an entire division with all its equipment in only 48 hours.

U.S. Army engineers duck for cover as a German artillery shell whistles overhead. They had been lowering an inflated pontoon into the Rhine.

A U.S. Third Army engineering crew joins together sections of a steel treadway bridge.

Engineers wait for another section of a Bailey bridge to be brought up and fitted into place.

A MARVEL OF SYNCHRONIZED TEAMWORK

"It was almost like maneuvers," said one observer of the engineers' bridge-building work on the Rhine. But the smooth operation was the result of long practice in synchronized teamwork.

While one gang of engineers lowered strings of inflated pontoons into the water, other teams in boats pushed the pontoon links into place. No sooner were the pontoons in position than other engineers began bolting on the treadway. The task of assembling the bridges went so fast that the engineers sometimes astounded themselves. One treadway bridge, scheduled to be finished in 36 hours, was opened for traffic in just nine hours.

With bridges in place, trucks carrying men and matériel of the U.S. Ninth Army roll across the Rhine, heading inland to seal off German escape routes.

Seventh Army GIs pile out of an assault boat and scramble up the muddy east bank of the Rhine near Worms.

4

Aiming at the heart of German industry
Hitler's obsession with miracles
"Go like hell. Don't stop."
An armored division 72 miles long
Tank crews with champagne hangovers
Clamping shut the giant pincers
The murderous 88s of Flak Alley
The baroque surrender of Lieutenant Ernst
Capturing towns by telephone
"The strangest battlefield I have ever seen"
Telling the Germans about Robert E. Lee
Finding a robin's-egg blue Mercedes
"A field marshal does not become a prisoner"

In the last days of March 1945, even as Field Marshal Montgomery expanded his *Plunder* bridgehead at Wesel, Allied forces were attacking at numerous points on the long battle front. Although the battle for the Rhine had by this time been won, many of these attacks were aimed at closing out that campaign.

Having already established a bridgehead at Oppenheim, General Patton's forces now jumped the river at Boppard and St. Goar, where the troops crossed in the face of cliffs 400 feet high. "The impossible place is usually the least well defended," Patton later explained. To Patton's right, General Patch concluded the Saar-Palatinate campaign by sending two divisions of his Seventh Army across the Rhine near the city of Worms. And to Patch's right, the French First Army began crossing the Rhine at Speyer and Germersheim. These moves established the Allies so widely on the east bank of the Rhine that the west bank, once so bitterly contested, was relegated to the status of a rear area.

But a new phase of the battle for Germany had just begun on the central front: General Bradley had launched Eisenhower's major drive to the Elbe River. A vital part of this plan involved Germany's industrial Ruhr region, which stretched eastward from the Rhine between General Simpson's Ninth Army in the Wesel bridgehead and General Hodges' First Army bridgehead at Remagen.

Under Ike's plan, both of these armies were to burst out of their bridgeheads, and their main bodies would thrust east toward the Elbe. But a large part of the First Army would slant northeast to link up behind the Ruhr with elements of the Ninth Army, which would swing southeast. Then, having enveloped the entire region in a giant bear hug, the two forces would squeeze to death the German armies that were trapped inside.

The Ruhr had long been a major concern of Allied planners. Before the War, the 2,000-square-mile region had possessed about 75 per cent of Germany's industry. Concentrated here were 18 great manufacturing cities; three of them—Essen, Düsseldorf and Dortmund—were each nearly as large as Pittsburgh. An immense coal deposit, 10 miles wide and 40 miles long, lay parallel to the Ruhr River; its 150 mines and 300,000 miners supplied the Reich with 69 per cent of its coal. Germans called the coal *Ruhrgeld,* or

ASSAULT ON "FORTRESS RUHR"

Ruhr money, for most of it was rich enough to make the metallurgical coke needed to convert iron ore into steel. Between the coal and the hydroelectric power generated at the Ruhr dams, the region's vast energy supply was sufficient to run more than 2,500 factories.

Manning the blast furnaces, drop forges, power lathes, steam presses, grinding wheels and finishing treadles was a labor force numbering some five million. The workers lived in a great jumble of urban neighborhoods whose narrow streets ended at slag heaps, railyards and factory gates. The grimy sprawl covered so much of the region that the towns and cities often merged into one another. Indeed, the northern part of the Ruhr was so densely developed that a person could travel its 50-mile length by streetcar.

With the outbreak of war, the Ruhr inevitably became a primary target for the Royal Air Force. RAF Air Chief Marshal Arthur Harris, known as "Bomber" Harris for his unshakable belief that strategic bombing could bring Germany to its knees, launched his first raid on the region in March 1942, hitting Essen with a 211-plane attack. Later, the biggest bombs ever carried by the RAF, each weighing 10,000 pounds, were dropped on three Ruhr River dams in an attempt—only partly successful—to cut off the hydroelectric power vital to the region's industry.

By the start of the Allies' Rhineland campaign in January of 1945, each of the Ruhr cities had been bombed dozens of times; Essen alone had been hit by 272 raids. And now the aerial attacks were stepped up even further. In a March 11 raid on Essen, 1,079 planes dropped 5,000 tons of bombs. The next day 1,108 planes hit Dortmund with 5,487 tons of explosives. Special targets were the 18 railroad bridges and viaducts that linked the Ruhr to the rest of Germany. By the 21st of March, 15 of the railroad bridges serving the region had been knocked out.

Yet strategic bombing had its limitations. After every raid, the people of the Ruhr had put out the fires, repaired the furnaces and restarted the assembly lines. Though the mighty raids cut into the output of the Ruhr, much of the damage was once again temporary, and the factories were soon producing great amounts of war matériel.

Obviously, the only sure way to put the Ruhr out of business for good was to occupy it. Accordingly, Allied strategists as early as 1942 had drafted various plans for the conquest of the region as a logical extension of the invasion of Normandy. The bear-hug plan eventually selected was part of an all-out Allied offensive along the entire front from Holland to the Swiss border. Within a few days, the whole Allied line of seven armies, totaling about four million men, would be on the move.

The Allies were ready. Their 85 combat divisions were without doubt better trained and better equipped than any force of comparable size in history. They were supported by massive air forces—now beginning to run out of targets. The Allied supply services had broken most of the bottlenecks and logjams and were delivering daily to each division something on the order of 500 tons of matériel. With the end of the War in sight, and with the weather improving, troop morale was high.

The Americans always griped about life in the Army—griping seemed to be a GI reflex—but now they were finding the War strangely tolerable. The policy of sending men to the rear for rest and rehabilitation had given some GIs a chance to go off on pass, and they had enjoyed rubbernecking visits to Rheims, Paris and the Riviera. Even at the front line, things were looking up. Shipments of cigarettes and mail deliveries were increasing. The combat troops were getting copies of the Army publications *Yank* and *Stars and Stripes,* which told them about the war they were fighting.

And there were new benefits to being the victors. Now that they were conquering enemy territory instead of liberating the countries of allies, they often slept in houses, apartments, taverns, hotels and even sumptuous villas; once a town fell to them, their billeting parties had only to select a good spot, tell the German inhabitants " 'Raus!'' ("Out!") and they were in. But discipline was becoming a problem. Many GIs violated orders against looting; they stole and mailed home cameras, silverware and assorted bric-a-brac. Incidents of rape by GIs were on the increase.

On the German side of the front line, the specter of defeat loomed ever larger. With rail and road transportation disrupted by Allied air raids, most Wehrmacht units were short of ammunition, gasoline and even food. As they retreated, the German soldiers found civilian morale as shaky as their own, with defeatist talk rampant. The troops were surprised and angered by the chilly reception they received from their own countrymen in some towns and villages; the citizens feared that their arrival would attract destructive air raids.

In fact, Germany's prospects were even more bleak than the soldiers could have known. The command situation along the Rhine was chaotic. Field Marshal Albert Kesselring, Commander in Chief West, wrote that he repeatedly informed Hitler that "the situation in the West had deteriorated too far to be effectively remedied." The Führer seemed to understand; at least he did not argue the point. Nonetheless, Kesselring had the impression that Hitler "was literally obsessed with the idea of some miraculous salvation, that he clung to it like a drowning man to a straw."

By now German communications were in such confusion that the Allies had a better idea than Kesselring did of the number of troops under his command. By actual count, the Wehrmacht had lost a quarter of a million men captured on the Western Front since the beginning of the Rhineland battles in February, and Allied intelligence estimates placed the total number of Germans killed or wounded at about 60,000 men. Intelligence reckoned that all the German effectives put together would make no more than 26 normal-sized divisions, or about 1.3 million men—one third the Allied strength.

Yet in spite of the Wehrmacht's desperate plight, the Allies had several reasons to believe that the coming battle for the Ruhr would still be a stern test. For one thing, the Germans were defending the heartland of their country now. Even if the hopelessness of their situation prompted some to lay down their arms, there were others who would fight to the death for the fatherland. So it had been in the Rhineland.

Then too, the terrain of the Ruhr strongly favored the defenders. The region was a landscape of picturesque streams, thick evergreen groves, steep ridges and sturdy stone farmhouses, where a few determined defenders could stall a sizable force of advancing riflemen and armor.

The industrial north was far more dangerous. The thick-walled factories and the bomb-wrecked houses were potential redoubts for snipers or tank-killing *Panzerfaust* teams. Overturned streetcars formed natural roadblocks. A standing wall of a house or church could hide a tank. Doorways could—and often would—contain booby traps. Wherever the Germans chose to fight, the Ruhr might soak up Allied soldiers like a sponge.

Another concern for the Allies was the German officer in command of Army Group B, charged with defense of the Ruhr: Field Marshal Walther Model. At the age of 54, Model was the Wehrmacht's youngest field marshal, and perhaps more than any other senior officer in the field he had Hitler's confidence. Model was one of the group of pro-Nazi

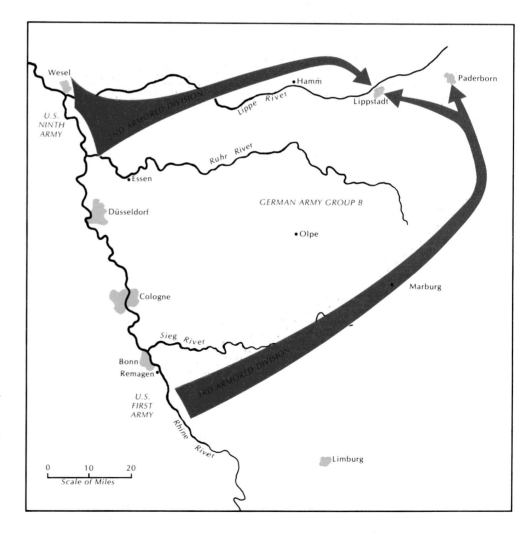

The plan for the encirclement and reduction of the Ruhr pocket was practically a textbook example of the classic double envelopment. Units of the U.S. First Army, led by the 3rd Armored Division, were to break out of their bridgehead at Remagen on March 25, race 70 miles east and then swing northeast. Ninth Army units, led by the 2nd Armored, were to plunge east from Wesel to meet the 3rd, trapping German Army Group B between them.

officers who rose in the decade of the 1930s to gain high rank in the German Army alongside the conservative generals of the Prussian aristocracy. Aggressive and ruthless, a master of improvisation, he had distinguished himself earlier in the War as an Army commander on the Eastern Front. In August of 1944, Hitler had sent him to France to restore the German front and to halt the Allied advance. Although he had failed to break the Allied line in the Battle of the Bulge, he had fared much better at Arnhem and along the Roer River, and he still basked in the Führer's esteem.

Model was so self-confident that he often disagreed with Hitler, a practice that had cost many generals their jobs. For one thing, he vigorously questioned Hitler's decision to stand and fight west of the Rhine. Repeatedly he had asked the Führer to rescind his order to "hold at all costs," recommending instead that as many as 20 divisions be withdrawn to prepare the Rhine River defenses. But Hitler had refused his requests, and Model had loyally fought where he stood.

Now, as the Ruhr battle was taking shape, an officer close to Model later reported, "like all senior commanders he faced an insoluble dilemma. As a highly qualified officer he saw the hopelessness of further resistance, but on the other hand he was bound in duty and honor to his superiors and subordinates." Hitler had promised Model help from a new force to be called the Twelfth Army if he could just hold the Allies at arm's length for a few more weeks. Model hoped that the Twelfth Army would arrive in time, but he was prepared to die fighting for a lost cause.

Currently, Model's Army Group B was a far cry from the crack force that had attacked in the Ardennes. Its main striking arm in that campaign, the Sixth Panzer Army, had been detached and sent east. Model retained the Fifth Panzer Army, but it had been badly mauled in the Bulge. He also had the bulk of the Fifteenth Army and two corps of the First Parachute Army, which had been driven south by Montgomery's *Plunder* forces. Additionally, about 100,000 Luftwaffe antiaircraft and service troops were assigned to his sector, putting the total number of defenders well above 300,000. Finally, Model hoped for help from Army Group H, deployed to the north of him under General Johannes Blaskowitz, and from SS General Paul Hausser and his Army Group G, holding the front to the south.

In the Ruhr, Model faced a difficult choice. Before positioning his troops, he had to guess how the Allies would attack. He knew that with strong bridgeheads at Wesel and Remagen, the Allies had no reason to mount further crossings of the Rhine and launch a direct frontal assault on the Ruhr. But would the Americans launch a double-pronged attack from Wesel and Remagen and then try to encircle the entire district? Or would they merely break out of their bridgeheads and capture the east bank of the Rhine?

Model guessed that they would take the river route; in the past the Allied strategy—unlike the Wehrmacht's, which favored a strong armor strike deep into enemy territory—usually called for only shallow breakthroughs, and consolidation of those gains before further advances. Accordingly, Model placed most of his troops in position to block any riverside drive and spread the rest of his men thin—much too thin—along the northern and southern flanks of the Ruhr.

The first thrust of the Ruhr offensive began before dawn on March 25, while Montgomery was still expanding his Wesel bridgehead. Eighty miles to the south, General Hodges shot seven of his First Army divisions due east from the Remagen bridgehead, aiming for the Dill River 45 miles distant.

This sector was defended by the German Fifteenth Army under Colonel General Gustav-Adolph von Zangen. The Fifteenth, none too strong to begin with, had just been further weakened; Field Marshal Model, on orders from Kesselring, had dispatched its two strongest units, the 11th Panzer Division and the 6th SS Mountain Division, south to counterattack the surprise Rhine crossing by General Patton's Third Army. Nevertheless, the Germans put up a stiff early fight in several areas. North of Remagen, where Model had stacked his defenses against a drive up the east bank of the Rhine, the Germans inflicted heavy punishment on the U.S. 1st Infantry Division and two columns of armor.

But the U.S. divisions, aided by fighter-bombers, were too strong to be held back for long. By the end of the first day, American armor had broken through German lines. Some German units began falling back to the north behind the Sieg River, and others retreated to the east. By the end of the second day, tanks of the 7th Armored Division had driven 50 miles east and captured 12,500 German soldiers.

The swift American advance threatened the town of Limburg, 20 miles east of the Rhine and 30 miles south of the

Sieg; here, five good roads branched north toward the Ruhr. This emergency prompted Kesselring to change his plans; he ordered Model to reassign the southbound 6th SS Mountain Division to the defense of Limburg.

The 6,000 men of the mountain division turned back toward Limburg. But they had run out of gasoline for their trucks and had to march the last 30 miles. When the first units reached Limburg late on March 26, they found that American tanks were already in the town.

The SS units were deployed piecemeal as they arrived during the night, building a hasty defense line astride the autobahn that ran south to Frankfurt. The next day the Americans attacked shortly after noon, and the issue was decided quickly. A combat command of the U.S. 9th Armored Division knifed through the Germans' defenses and had driven 15 miles beyond by nightfall.

That afternoon, Lieut. General Gustav Hoehne, commander of the 79th Corps, which now included the 6th SS Mountain Division, radioed Kesselring that the incoming Americans at Limburg were pressing hard and that their tanks had broken through to his rear. Could he withdraw east of the Limburg autobahn?

Kesselring's answer was no. But the following morning Hoehne decided to disobey orders. He had lost contact with his mountain division; a report from his only surviving division, the 276th Infantry, informed him that collapse was imminent, and his own headquarters was under fire from U.S. reconnaissance units. So the general ordered a withdrawal and headed east himself with 30 members of his staff. Later Hoehne noted dryly, "Corps headquarters was no longer in position to exercise effective command."

During the battle for Limburg, the 6th SS Mountain Division had been reduced to about 2,000 men. Cut off to the west of the Limburg-Frankfurt autobahn, the troopers defended a succession of roadblocks there for the next two days, taking more casualties. Finally, during the night of March 30, they gave up the pointless struggle and began trying to filter back to the German lines.

As they headed east by a roundabout route, the SS troopers came across a U.S. field hospital and temporarily took it under control. Soon a story went out on the American grapevine that the SS had slaughtered the hospital staff and raped the nurses. This rumor—entirely false—may have

RASPBERRIES FOR THE FÜHRER

As the Allied armies pushed on into Germany, the troops passed up few opportunities to express their opinion of Adolf Hitler. The British and the Americans alike took malicious glee in defacing pictures of the Führer, hanging him in effigy or otherwise deriding him.

The comics among the GIs specialized in doing imitations of Hitler, by holding combs under their noses for a mustache, sticking their arms out straight in the Nazi salute and screaming madly at the top of their lungs. And the troops sang a dialect song made popular by Spike Jones and his band, sounding off with a loud Bronx cheer after each "Heil": "Ven der Führer says, Ve is der Master Race, / Ve Heil! Heil! Right in der Führer's face."

A GI burlesques Hitler atop Nuremberg's Nazi Party Congress Stadi

On Adolf Hitler Bridge in Coblenz, a soldier thumbs his nose at the Führer's name.

A GI draws Hitler's face on a "valentine" for use as a target on February 14, 1945.

An MP tightens the noose on a crude bust of Hitler decorating a pontoon bridge.

A Canadian soldier "drowns" Hitler in a street puddle.

A soldier bayonets a Hitler photo lying on the pavement.

added to the ferocity with which infantrymen of the 5th and 71st Infantry Divisions hunted down the SS men, killing 500 before permitting the last 800 to surrender. But the GIs needed no special encouragement. SS troops had an evil reputation among Americans for atrocities such as the Malmédy massacre in Belgium, and in many units there was a tacit agreement to take no SS prisoners.

The collapse of Hoehne's corps severed the last contact between Army Group B and Army Group G to the south. Only one of the German Fifteenth Army's three corps was left, for a second was beating a hasty retreat to the east in time to escape the closing trap. By March 28, Hodges' First Army had captured the little university town of Marburg, 65 miles east of the Rhine, in the process taking 16,000 German prisoners. The whole southern border of the Ruhr now lay wide open to the Americans.

General Bradley ordered the First Army to wheel north from Marburg toward a linkup with the Ninth Army under General Simpson. Bradley's order went down to the VII Corps, commanded by Major General J. Lawton "Lightning Joe" Collins, who passed it along to the 3rd Armored Division. Major General Maurice Rose, commander of the 3rd Armored, was to lead the run north.

General Rose assigned the vanguard role to Colonel Robert L. Howze Jr., commander of the 3rd Armored's 36th Armored Infantry Regiment. Late on the night of March 28, Howze summoned his battalion commanders and briefed them on the new assignment for the next day. Standing before a map, the colonel pointed to a town that was more than 60 miles to the north and said, "Tomorrow morning you leave for Paderborn."

Lieut. Colonel Walter B. Richardson, the commander of Howze's tank force, could hardly believe his ears. "You mean get to Paderborn in one day?" he asked.

"Just go like hell," Howze said. "Get the high ground at the Paderborn airport. Don't stop." The rest of the 3rd Armored Division would follow.

On that same day, the 28th of March, Field Marshal Montgomery issued orders for his Twenty-first Army Group to break out of its deep, wide bridgehead around Wesel and head east and northeast. At this point, Montgomery still believed that his army group was to play the leading role in the Allied drive to the Elbe River. But that evening Montgomery received the controversial message in which Eisenhower announced his radical change in plans for the last offensive—including the fact that Montgomery would have to turn over the U.S. Ninth Army to Bradley. Wrote Eisenhower: "As soon as you and Bradley have joined hands in the Kassel-Paderborn area, Ninth Army will revert to Bradley's command. He will then be responsible for occupying and mopping up the Ruhr. Your army group will protect Bradley's northern flank."

For the time being, nothing changed in the field. Simpson's Ninth Army drove ahead on a broad front. In the van was the powerful "Hell on Wheels" 2nd Armored Division, its vehicles forming a column 72 miles long. Though the bulk of the division averaged only two miles an hour, its reconnaissance units raced on, bypassing German resistance, disrupting German communications, cutting the main supply routes between the Ruhr and Berlin—and moving so rapidly that they ran off their maps. Resourceful officers began using tattered old Baedekers and the escape maps that Allied pilots carried with them in case they were shot down over Germany.

Meanwhile, to the south, Lieut. Colonel Richardson, leading his battalion north toward Paderborn from Marburg, found the going easy at first. He set off at 6 a.m. on March 29, with several jeeps leading his 23 tanks, 20 of them carrying infantrymen on their decks. All day long they raced north in columns. Without stopping, they knocked out a passenger train and rolled through several undefended military installations. Through the eastern reaches of the Ruhr they rumbled, passing farmsteads and small villages that huddled in the folds of wooded hills. They saw many dismayed villagers but met only sporadic resistance.

By dusk Richardson had traveled 35 miles. As he neared a road that led to Brilon, he got a radio order from General Rose to take that town, in which a small German force was holed up; the general wanted it cleared out to avoid any trouble on the flank. So Richardson sent his main body to deal with Brilon and, retaining a few vehicles for security, went on ahead to look for the route to Paderborn.

He spent an hour wandering about in open country before a helpful civilian told him that the best road to Paderborn lay just ahead to the north. By then it was dark, and the spring chill had given way to a thick fog. Visibility was so bad that Richardson got out of his jeep to guide the vehicles on foot. Just then he heard the rumble of tanks behind him; the force he had sent to take Brilon had finished and was rejoining him. His advance party moved on, and Richardson signaled the tanks forward with his flashlight. The lead tank came growling along so close behind him that it bumped him. Richardson frantically signaled a halt. The first tank stopped short—causing a series of rear-end collisions.

Richardson climbed up on the lead tank in order to berate the crew, and poking his flashlight inside the turret, saw an appalling sight: The tank commander was staring back up at him bleary-eyed, with a champagne bottle clutched in each hand. Then Richardson spotted the bat-

An American soldier looks over a captured wooden dummy of a tank set atop a small armored vehicle. Such imitations were used with some success to confuse British and American reconnaissance planes.

talion medical officer, who explained that they had found a warehouse full of champagne in Brilon. With a big grin the doctor said, ''We ought to go back to Brilon.''

Richardson angrily issued some orders to nearby officers. ''Guide the tanks up the road. Throw the champagne out and keep all the hatches open.'' The cold and damp would sober up the men fast enough.

At midnight Richardson checked his speedometer. The task force had gone 45 miles in a single day and the only casualties were a batch of hangovers. He stopped his column, told his troopers to gas up, eat something and get a few hours' sleep. The next morning, Richardson knew, they would be in for a fight, for just 15 miles ahead lay Paderborn, and nearby there was a German tank school and an SS panzer replacement training center.

By the time Richardson's task force stopped for the night, Field Marshal Model, at his headquarters at the village of Olpe in the south-central Ruhr, realized that the encircle-

U.S. Ninth Army soldiers, fighting their way into Essen in mid-April, look for snipers in the bomb-ravaged Krupp armaments works. At the time, the German radio was boasting that thousands of civilian snipers lay in wait for the Americans among the city's shattered factories; although the GIs took the threat seriously, no such resistance appeared.

ment of the region was imminent, and he sent Kesselring a long teletype message pleading for permission to withdraw Army Group B while the way was still open. The message said, "To continue the defense in the position is absurd, as such a defense could not even pin down enemy forces."

Model proposed a withdrawal and a limited counterattack to protect it: Some of his panzers would cut off the bulk of the U.S. 3rd Armored Division as it came up to join Richardson near Paderborn. Kesselring approved Model's attack plan immediately. But he vetoed the withdrawal request, insisting that the fight for the Ruhr was vital to the Third Reich. Model unleashed his counterattack early on March 30. The tanks and infantry of General Fritz Bayerlein's 53rd Corps—the only remaining corps of the Fifteenth Army—would strike along the line of the 3rd Armored Division's advance, thrusting here and there in search of a soft spot. At the same time, the SS forces around Paderborn would attack to the south, hitting the 3rd Armored's vanguard.

Richardson, at the head of the advance, was assaulted soon after dawn by SS trainees and panzers from Paderborn. He immediately lost two Sherman tanks in a crossroads clash with German Panther tanks. A few miles farther on, Richardson's force met a fierce attack by a force of SS men and about 60 Panther and Tiger tanks. Richardson called for tactical air support, but the heavy cloud cover following the fog of the night before made air support impossible.

That afternoon, the task force fought its way into the town of Kerchborchen, six miles from Paderborn. Richardson had received a radio warning that strong German attacks to his rear, all of them by Bayerlein's corps, had cut him off. He had no choice but to hold here until General Rose and the rest of the 3rd Armored Division broke through to his aid.

Toward dusk on March 30, Rose was moving forward at the head of another task force. But small-arms fire from a roadside woods separated the general and a few vehicles from the main body. Then Rose saw German tanks looming out of the darkness. Corporal Glen H. Shaunce, Rose's jeep driver, tried to gun the vehicle into the woods to dodge the enemy armor, but a Tiger tank barred the way.

A soldier in the turret motioned with his burp gun. Rose dismounted with his aide, Major Robert Bellinger, and driver Shaunce. Standing in front of the tank, Bellinger and Shaunce carefully unbuckled their pistol belts and let them drop. As Rose started to do the same, something alarmed the German holding the burp gun; he fired. Bellinger and Shaunce dived for a ditch—and got away in the confusion that followed. But Maury Rose pitched forward, dead.

By daylight on March 31, General Bayerlein's counterattack had petered out as the U.S. 8th, 9th and 104th Infantry Divisions—the rest of the VII Corps—moved up to bolster the 3rd Armored's advance. With his rear once again secure, Richardson could move out for Paderborn. He and his men arrived on the outskirts early that day and immediately had another battle on their hands. The SS troopers came at them with tanks, tank destroyers and the antitank grenade launchers called Panzerfausts. They seemed determined to fight to the death.

The clash at the tank school inspired an urgent telephone call from VII Corps commander Lightning Joe Collins to General Simpson at U.S. Ninth Army headquarters in the north. Collins explained that Richardson's column of the 3rd Armored was meeting with fanatic SS opposition at the tank school and that it might take days for the 3rd Armored to fight its way through Paderborn and establish contact with the Ninth Army. So Collins put a question: Could Simpson turn a combat command of the Ninth Army's 2nd Armored Division southeast from Beckum, where it now had its vanguard troops, toward Lippstadt, a little town 25 miles west of Paderborn? Collins, for his part, would split off a force from the 3rd Armored and send it to meet the Ninth Army unit at Lippstadt. The Ruhr pocket would be slightly smaller at the northeast corner, but the linkup could be accomplished that much sooner, freeing more units of the First and Ninth Armies for a fast push east.

General Simpson agreed at once and on Easter, April 1, the new orders went out to the 2nd and 3rd Armored Divisions. Elements of both outfits set out in the darkness for the rendezvous at Lippstadt.

The lead element of the troops dispatched by the 2nd Armored Division was a company of new Pershing tanks and some infantry under First Lieutenant William Dooley, who had orders to get his outfit to Lippstadt as fast as he could. That meant a 50-mile thrust southeast, and Dooley had to grope most of the way in the dark.

The same night, the 3rd Armored Division responded to

the change in plan with a reinforced battalion of tanks and infantry under Lieut. Colonel Matthew W. Kane. Kane's vehicles left the outskirts of Paderborn moving single file, a tank company in the lead and the battalion headquarters' half-track behind it. Captain Foster F. Flegeal, standing in the half-track, manned the vehicle's .50-caliber machine gun and strained his eyes to keep sight of the blackout lights on the tail of the vehicle in front.

Soon after daybreak, Kane's battalion approached Lippstadt and ran into a defended roadblock. The column halted as the tanks of the forward element prepared to clear the obstacle. Then, from the right, a column of about 10 German trucks and armored cars roared out of a side road, obviously intending to cut through the American line. Captain Flegeal opened up with his .50-caliber machine gun, and so did every other American gunner. Streams of tracer bullets riddled the German column, and tank shells blasted into it with great gouts of flame. One after another, the German vehicles were stopped dead, knocked over and set ablaze, and the German survivors crawled out, hands raised in surrender. Captain Flegeal detached a group of medics to take care of the wounded, then pressed on toward Lippstadt.

Meanwhile, the 2nd Armored column had reached the northern outskirts of Lippstadt, and Lieutenant Dooley sent a platoon of tanks under Second Lieutenant Donald E. Jacobsen into town to look around. Jacobsen's tankers pushed through town to the eastern edge. From there they saw a distant column of tanks and armored vehicles approaching from the southeast, trailing a plume of dust. Jacobsen deployed his tanks and got ready to fire.

The approaching column was Kane's 3rd Armored, its M5 light tanks in the lead. And when Kane saw tanks on the edge of Lippstadt, he instantly halted his column and also fanned them out in combat formation. To Kane, the new Pershings in Lippstadt looked like German tanks with their unfamiliar silhouette and muzzle brakes on the gun tubes.

There was a nervous standoff while the two outfits studied each other. Finally both groups realized that they were staring at friendly armor. The envelopment of the Ruhr had been completed.

The GIs mingled for a few minutes. There were cheers, some ribald jokes and a great sense of relief that there had been no fight for the town. The men of the 3rd Armored Di-

vision began calling the Ruhr pocket the "Rose Pocket" in honor of their fallen General Rose. Trapped in that pocket was most of Field Marshal Model's command—considerably more than 300,000 men.

With the Ruhr sealed off, General Eisenhower reassessed the Allied position, and Ike could only be delighted with what he saw. Already the Saar and Silesia in the east, Ger-

The empty streets and crumbling buildings of Soest are patrolled by men of the 95th Infantry Division. A key rail junction, Soest was fiercely defended by the 116th Panzer Division; the town finally fell on April 6 after a punishing attack by U.S. fighter-bombers that killed 300 Germans.

many's two other industrial regions, had fallen. Now that the Ruhr was enveloped, Eisenhower concluded that the enemy's few "remaining industries, dispersed over the central area of the country, could not possibly support his armies still attempting to fight. Communications were badly broken and no Nazi senior commander could ever be sure that his orders would reach the troops for whom they were intended. While in many areas there were troops capable of putting up fierce and stubborn local resistance, only on the northern and southern flanks of the great Western Front were there armies of sufficient size to do more than delay Allied advances."

The task of liquidating the Ruhr pocket was left to General Bradley and his Twelfth Army Group. Bradley first had to figure out how many units were needed to do the job and how many to assign to the drive east. Counting the Ninth

Army, which Montgomery would return to his command on April 4, Bradley would have 48 divisions. He decided to leave 18 behind to mop up the Ruhr.

These formations, grouped in four corps, would close in on the Germans from three sides, with the Ninth Army divisions attacking the northern side of the pocket and the First Army divisions assaulting the eastern and southern sides. Another U.S. army, the Fifteenth, was brought up to guard the west bank of the Rhine against any spoiling raids from the other side and to conduct raids of its own to keep the German forces pinned down.

Inside the pocket, Field Marshal Model saw his position deteriorating steadily. On April 1, the day he learned of the American linkup at Lippstadt, Model received another piece of bad news from Kesselring. As he had suspected, there was no sign of the promised help from the Twelfth Army; that force was just assembling along the Elbe. The Führer's orders, Kesselring said, were for Army Group B to hold the "Fortress Ruhr" to the last man.

April 2 and April 3 brought increasing American pressure all around the Ruhr—and a succession of urgent meetings at Army Group B headquarters. Model's staff officers told him that resistance could be maintained for no more than two weeks. They also persisted in discussing when and how the command might surrender. Though Model listened to this subversive talk he refused to consider surrendering. It was a German Army tradition that field marshals did not surrender, and Model himself had publicly damned the only field marshal who had thus disgraced the Army and the fatherland: Friedrich Paulus, commander of the Sixth Army at Stalingrad.

Orders for the last-ditch stand were circulated to local commanders and civilian authorities. The people of the Ruhr were called upon to contribute food and medical supplies and to resist the American invaders—an SS general demanded nothing less than a region-wide "model of guerrilla resistance." Swift punishment was threatened for anyone who surrendered or sheltered Wehrmacht deserters or cooperated with Allied troops. But neither the threats nor the appeals would prove notably successful; materially and emotionally, the population had little left to give.

On April 4, when the U.S. Ninth Army was finally returned to General Bradley's command, the fighting grew heavier. Troops of three divisions were battling among the factories on the northern edge of the Ruhr. U.S. tanks made a deep penetration near Soest in the northeastern Ruhr, and a second American column thrust across the Lippe River near the rail hub of Hamm in the northwestern Ruhr.

But the GIs found the going rough. This was Flak Alley—a route taken so often by Allied bombers that it was defended by 2,400 antiaircraft guns. As the Germans had demonstrated earlier, the high-velocity 88mm and 128mm antiaircraft guns were murderous antitank weapons, and they soon slowed the American drives from the north.

On the eastern side of the pocket, Ninth Army units drove the remnants of the German Fifteenth Army out of the town of Winterberg and pushed on beyond. Beside them the U.S. 99th Division from the First Army struggled forward over rugged terrain, advancing 10 miles in four days, capturing 18 towns and 2,000 prisoners.

Then the 99th Division reached Iserlohn, a substantial town nestled in the Lenne mountains. The GIs ringed the town, which was defended by the SS and troops of the once-formidable Panzer Lehr Division, and an American lieutenant went forward on a tank that was equipped with a public-address system. In flawless German, the lieutenant boomed out over his loudspeaker, "Soldiers in Iserlohn, your situation is hopeless. You are completely encircled.

A 15-year-old German soldier bursts into tears after being taken prisoner near Giessen. Though many youngsters, hastily recruited as Germany scraped the bottom of its manpower barrel, lost their boyish bravery after firing a few shots, others fought doggedly until disabled or killed.

Major General Harry L. Twaddle (center), commander of the Ninth Army's Task Force Twaddle, interviews Hitler's former Vice Chancellor Franz von Papen (right) and his son, Captain Franz, Jr. (left), after their capture in the Ruhr pocket. "I wish this war were over," the old man complained when U.S. troops burst into his country hideaway as he was finishing dinner. A GI snapped back, "So do 11 million other guys!"

Lay down your arms and surrender at once or we will annihilate you with artillery fire.''

More than 400 Germans heeded the call, throwing down their weapons and raising their hands. But a German lieutenant named Ernst was intent on a surrender befitting an officer of one of the Wehrmacht's most decorated divisions. He brought his three heavy tank destroyers, 128mm weapons mounted on Tiger-tank chassis, into careful alignment in the town square and elevated the barrels. Then he had the men of his depleted company form ranks. After shaking hands with each man, he called his troops to attention and gave a short speech. Finally, Lieutenant Ernst executed a smart about-face, saluted an astonished American officer and formally surrendered, *korrekt* to the end.

On the southern flank of the Ruhr, the Americans had an easy time in some sectors and ran into staunch resistance in others. The defense was especially tough along the routes that Model had originally believed the Americans would take in breaking out of their Remagen bridgehead. The U.S. 13th Armored Division drew one of these routes; its assignment was to fight northward along the east bank of the Rhine and clear the enemy out of the part of Cologne that lay on the east side of the river.

As the 13th approached Cologne, it ran into remnants of the German 3rd Parachute Division manning 88mm antiaircraft cannon. The paratroopers fired into the advancing American tanks, and one after another, tanks blew up in flames or lurched to a halt, their tracks snapping like broken rubber bands. But the Americans had still more tanks, and gradually they overwhelmed the courageous defenders.

To the southeast of the 13th Armored, the U.S. 78th Division stormed across the Sieg River in plywood boats. As the infantrymen hammered out a bridgehead on the north side of the river, the German defense collapsed. Soon the division was advancing so fast toward Wuppertal, 50 miles to the northeast, that its headquarters had to be moved almost daily to keep up. The advance could have been even faster had the road not been jammed by German stragglers and German trucks and tanks abandoned for lack of fuel.

Soon after crossing the Sieg, the 78th began taking towns by telephone. As advance patrols raced into an undefended town, the troops quickly searched out the local telephone exchange. A German-speaking GI would have the operator raise the next town and demand to speak to the *Bürgermeister* or to the local military commander. The GI would inform him, ''This is the American Army. Your town is next on our list for wipe-out if you don't surrender. So get the white sheets out!''

The phone-call ultimatums were surprisingly effective. More often than not, the Americans found, on approach-

ing the next town, dozens of windows displaying the white flags of surrender.

While the fighting for the Ruhr fizzled or flared in the north, the east and the south, the soldiers of the U.S. Fifteenth Army sat on the west bank of the Rhine with little to do but look out for German forays that never came. Periodically, units of the Fifteenth were ordered across the Rhine to test the German riverside defenses or to establish forward listening posts for elements of the First and Ninth Armies, which were advancing along the east bank of the river.

In one such operation, 140 men of the veteran U.S. 82nd Airborne Division went across in assault boats north of Cologne at Hitdorf. Quickly they ran into a devastating counterattack by a large force of enemy tanks and infantry. For a time it appeared that the Americans would be wiped out to a man. But reinforcements crossed the Rhine to their aid, and artillery on the west bank slowed the German attack. Even so, only 28 of the 140 paratroopers returned unscathed—all the rest were killed, wounded or missing.

Unchastened by the 82nd's fiasco, a 20-man patrol from the inexperienced 94th Infantry Division crossed the river—and got away with nothing but a bad scare. The infantrymen landed in the middle of a heavy concentration of 37mm antiaircraft guns. Hastily they took cover in a house and were surrounded by German soldiers. That night, a German called out, urging the Americans to surrender. Staff Sergeant Jerome Fatora replied with hot lead. Then, as he later told it, "bazookas smashed the house and machine guns raked all the doors and windows. Next morning the Heinies battered the cellar entrance with *Panzerfausts*. We gave up all hope of escape.

"About 8 o'clock in the morning the Jerries, numbering 75 in all, rushed the house. Their lieutenant shouted to us in perfect English: 'Gentlemen' (all of a sudden he considered us gentlemen), 'you have five minutes to surrender.'"

Instead, Fatora's lieutenant shouted an ultimatum of his own: "Surrender to us. You are already caught in the center of a huge pincers."

The German thought that over for a moment. Then he complained, "But we must answer to superiors, and any-

way you will be prisoners of war for only a few days before you are freed by your comrades." The German gave the American lieutenant two minutes to make up his mind, and then shouted back, "Your time is up, gentlemen. Are you coming out?"

The American lieutenant finally muttered, "Yeah, we're coming out." The patrol was marched off into German captivity. But a few days later, just as the German had predicted, they were freed—by the U.S. 13th Armored Division.

By April 6, the American vise was crushing the Germans into a smaller and smaller perimeter. The only sizable battle was being fought for the heavily industrialized northwest corner, an area measuring 12 miles from north to south between the Lippe and Ruhr Rivers, and 60 miles west to east from the Rhine to the railroad center of Hamm. It was, according to General Friedrich von Mellenthin, chief of staff of the German Fifth Panzer Army, "the strangest battlefield I have ever seen."

In the Duisburg-Essen-Dortmund industrial complex, on the north side of the Ruhr, the heavy and repeated Allied bombings had created weird patterns of destruction. The high-explosive bombs and the fires set by incendiary bombs had seemingly wrecked no two structures in the same way, stripping the walls from some buildings, gutting other buildings while leaving the walls intact, and reducing still other buildings to rubble except for one or two walls. One GI who fought in the ruins reported seeing a building that was almost totally destroyed except for a drainpipe that reached to the third-story level, where it supported a bathtub with a long-handled scrub brush still dangling over the side. Other soldiers remembered the empty window frames on freestanding walls; they were like the eye sockets of human skulls. The Americans recalled the pathetic possessions of former residents—broken chairs, a kitchen range with its legs skyward like a stricken beast, the bright bit of color in the drab junk that turned out to be a child's doll.

There was the smell, too—the peculiar sweet-sour stink of sewer gas, decay and death. Under the piles of rubble lay the bodies of innumerable people killed by the bombs. The only record of their presence, besides the stench, was the usual German cross atop the heap, a faded bunch of flowers, and perhaps on the cross the words, "Hier liegen 25 Personen."

Some civilians still lived in the ruins. Hungry, thirsty, sick, they huddled in cellars while shells erupted all around them. In lulls in the fighting, or when the German defenders retreated to the next block of rubble, they ventured out with their hands up, waving anything white—a dirty towel, a fragment of a sheet.

But the German soldiers fought on and on. They were a mixed group—SS men, paratroopers and elements of the Fifth Panzer Army. Many of them died fighting to hold a slag heap or a cellar.

General Simpson of the Ninth Army wanted to end the irksome battle so he could press eastward. To clear the industrial corner he combined the 95th Infantry Division, the 8th Armored Division, the 15th Cavalry Group and a regiment from the 17th Airborne Division into a large task force under Major General Harry L. Twaddle. This battle group, designated Task Force Twaddle, joined in a coordinated attack along the Ruhr River on April 7.

Swiftly the Americans pushed on to Gelsenkirchen, a small factory town north of Essen. By April 8, Task Force

German women bring food and water to captured soldiers in a U.S. First Army prisoner-of-war cage. Although the POWs were entitled to a daily ration of 4,000 calories, the overtaxed Allied supply lines could not keep up with the tremendous influx of German troops, and local civilians were called upon to provide supplementary food.

Thousands of surrendered German soldiers mill about in a compound in the Ruhr. Among the captives were hundreds of uniformed women, some of whom the SS had pressed into service as "soldier comforters"—i.e., camp followers for the elite Nazi troopers.

Twaddle was fighting its way into Hamm, which had once held Germany's largest railroad-marshaling yard. On reaching the city, a platoon of the U.S. 95th Infantry Division had a bad moment when a column of German tanks and trucks emerged from the morning mist that hung over the nearby Lippe River. The Germans opened fire. Lieutenant Jack Baine, the platoon leader, deployed his men, and Private First Class George Hyatt let fly with a bazooka, hitting a lead truck, which happened to be laden with high explosives. A tremendous series of explosions stunned the GIs. When the dust settled, the entire German column had disappeared. After that, Task Force Twaddle took possession of Hamm with only scattered skirmishes.

Nine miles south of Hamm, at the town of Unna, the remnants of the German 116th Panzer Division greeted the U.S. 8th Armored Division with a rain of shells. The Americans responded with a fierce attack, supported by artillery and fighter planes. After a brisk two-hour fight, the 116th Panzer Division escaped to the south, leaving behind 160 prisoners, two tanks, four 88s and five smaller cannon. Later the same day another column of the 8th Armored rounded up the remnants of the 116th Panzer Division.

By April 11, the Germans were falling back rapidly in all quarters; the Ruhr pocket was reduced to an average diameter of about 16 miles. And April 14 was a big day for the Americans. They split the remaining pocket from north to south. In the industrial northeast they overran Mülheim, Oberhausen, Bochum and, best of all, Essen, the Ruhr's unofficial capital. For the most part, the Germans had withdrawn from these areas into the Ruhr interior, so the GIs took few prisoners. But they made one important catch: Alfred Krupp von Bohlen und Halbach, president of Germany's great Krupp works and a man high on the Allies' wanted list of war criminals.

After April 11, the Germans' dwindling defenses seemed likely to collapse at any minute. The Americans met with resistance only in Dortmund and a few other strong points. Every day more and more Germans were giving up. Most of the American divisions were collecting between 2,000 and 5,000 prisoners a day. A GI of the 78th Infantry Division left Wuppertal for his regimental collecting point with 68 prisoners; by the time he reached his destination, his bag of prisoners had swelled to 1,200.

General von Zangen and his Fifteenth Army staff surrendered on April 13. The next day, General Bayerlein, having finally received permission from Field Marshal Model to attempt a breakout, recognized that it was now impossible, and he too surrendered with the remnants of his 53rd Corps.

On April 13, the U.S. 75th and 95th Divisions cleared the approaches to Dortmund. By nightfall the 95th Division had taken the city by storm, and GIs roamed through the ruins rooting out a few hiding German soldiers. On April 14, GIs of the First Army's 8th Division fought past Hagen and linked up with a unit of the Ninth Army's XIX Corps, splitting the Ruhr pocket again into two segments. At once the Germans in both segments found themselves attacked and driven inward from yet another direction. Army Group B was swiftly dying.

On April 15, Field Marshal Model received under a flag of truce a courier bearing a carefully composed letter from an American general. The general was Matthew B. Ridgway, XVIII Airborne Corps commander, and his letter read:

"Neither history nor the military profession records any nobler character, any more brilliant master of warfare, any more dutiful subordinate of the state, than the American General, Robert E. Lee. Eighty years ago this month, his loyal command reduced in numbers, stripped of its means of effective fighting and completely surrounded by overwhelming forces, he chose an honorable capitulation.

"The same choice is now yours. In the light of a soldier's honor, for the reputation of the German officer corps, for the sake of your nation's future, lay down your arms at once. The German lives you will save are sorely needed to restore your people to their proper place in society. The German cities you will preserve are irreplaceable necessities for your people's welfare."

Model rejected the proposal that he surrender. But he had known that his battle would come to this grim end ever since April 1, when the American pincers had snapped shut at Lippstadt, and his staff's discussions of surrender had prompted him to think seriously of other alternatives. Now that organized resistance was pointless and indeed impossible, he had in mind a way out of his dilemma—an unorthodox way, to be sure, but not a dishonorable one.

A command that did not exist, Model reasoned, could not surrender; he decided to disband Army Group B in place.

On April 15, Model ordered that the youths and older men of the *Volkssturm,* or home guard, be issued discharge papers immediately and sent home. He also ordered that, as of April 17, when presumably all the remaining ammunition and other supplies would be distributed, support troops would be free to surrender. Thereafter, soldiers in combat units could decide for themselves whether to fight on, surrender or try to make their way home. By April 18, all resistance ended.

Now the stream of surrendering German soldiers became a flood. The Americans could accommodate all the prisoners only by hastily fencing them in open fields with barbed wire. Germans of all ranks and services surrendered: the old and the young, fliers and antiaircraft gunners, bewildered home guardsmen and SS troopers still arrogant in defeat, 22 generals and numerous highly placed civilians, Wehrmacht nurses and slow-moving groups of walking wounded. Some soldiers carried accordions or guitars, and some even brought their wives or girl friends. Some were downcast, some were happy.

When the final tally of prisoners was taken, the total came to 317,000 Germans—more troops than had surrendered to the Russians at Stalingrad. The cost of the campaign to the Ninth Army was 341 killed, 121 missing and about 2,000 wounded. The First Army's casualties were roughly three times higher.

But days passed and still there was no sign of Field Marshal Model. General Bradley offered a medal to whoever brought him in. Model's Mercedes-Benz—robin's-egg blue with red leather upholstery—was found empty deep in a forest by a detachment from the 8th Armored Division. The car was given to Bradley.

As it happened, Model had abandoned the telltale car in an effort to escape through American lines. After dissolving his army group, the field marshal had left his temporary headquarters near the southwestern Ruhr village of Schalksmühle, along with three staff officers and five soldiers. As the party moved stealthily through the ruins of the western Ruhr, the field marshal's aides repeatedly urged him to surrender, but he still would not consider it. "A field marshal," he said, still remembering Paulus at Stalingrad, "does not become a prisoner. Such a thing is just not possible."

During Model's wanderings, he chanced to meet a German sergeant, Walter Maxeiner. A thrice-wounded veteran of campaigns on both European fronts, Maxeiner had received his discharge on April 16 near Witten, and he and a few of his men were trying to make their way home when they spied the field marshal, seated on an 88mm gun carriage in the middle of his little party. "Model was holding his head in his hands," Maxeiner recalled. "We went up, asking what we should do. With great astonishment our young soldiers looked at the officers with the stripes on their pants and their medals. Never before had they been so close to 'big brass.'

"When Field Marshal Model, for that is who it was, saw us, he beckoned us over, asked where our homes were, our age and military careers. For some time he discussed my tour of duty on the Eastern Front with me. It turned out I had been in a unit under his command at the time."

Maxeiner then asked Model what he should do now. "He answered, 'Go home boys. The War is over for us.' With a serious mien, he shook hands with me and said, 'Good luck on the trip home, and tell your men not to lose courage and to continue to remain decent boys.'" Maxeiner and his companions continued on their furtive way.

Model, too, resumed his trek, and on April 21 he reached a wood near Duisburg. His party was weary, and Model's second adjutant, a colonel named Pilling, heard the field marshal ask in quiet despair, "What is left to a commander in defeat?" Then Model answered his own question: "In ancient times, they took poison."

A staff officer again urged Model to surrender. Once again Model said, "I simply cannot do it. The Russians have branded me a war criminal, and the Americans would be sure to turn me over to them for hanging."

Late in the afternoon of April 21, Model told Colonel Pilling, "My hour has come. Follow me." Model led his aide deep into the forest. There he drew his pistol from its holster and instructed Pilling, "You will bury me here."

Field Marshal Walther Model ended his life with a single shot. The battle for Fortress Ruhr was over.

THE RAMPAGING AMERICANS

An American tank shells German homes in the town of Geisselhardt, blasting and burning out snipers who had interrupted the Seventh Army's advance.

SPREADING EASTWARD LIKE AN INK BLOT

After the Allies crossed the Rhine in March 1945, the thin crust of German defenses crumbled, and the front line spread east like a huge ink blot. From the Rhine to the Elbe, four American armies—the First, Third, Seventh and Ninth—hounded a beaten and disorganized enemy in one of the swiftest, most stunning pursuits in military history.

Everywhere, powerful American task forces made up of tanks and infantry were on the loose, rampaging over the flat German countryside and rolling along the convenient superhighways that Adolf Hitler had built for his Wehrmacht. The task forces simply drove east as fast as they could. "The footsloggers," said an infantry commander, "became marathon runners."

Whenever pockets of German resistance appeared, the tanks would attempt to knock them out with air and artillery support. But if this took too long, the task forces would simply bypass the strong points and leave them for the infantry to mop up—occasioning a sour slogan from foot soldiers: "bypass, haul ass and yell for the infantry."

In a single day, the 35th Division of the U.S. Ninth Army moved 220 miles due east. Gütersloh, Oerlinghausen, Detmold, Gestorf—the names of the towns and villages went on and on. "When we go into those pretty little towns, we don't aspire to damage anything," said a battalion commander. "But if German soldiers are there, everything that can be burned is burned and every building destroyed." Woe to those homes that failed to display a white flag of surrender. "We don't knock on the door and say please," said another officer. "We rip its windows with machine-gun fire."

The speed and savagery of the advance excited even those battle-weary dogfaces who had spent eight straight months in the line. The GIs looked forward to the last fights ahead, and they relished the moments in their headlong advance when they passed columns of German prisoners plodding in the opposite direction. A reporter for the armed forces magazine *Yank* heard one GI growl: "Why don't you goose-step now, you sonavabitches!"

Flushed with success, a Ninth Army soldier nails up a sign near the town of Lippstadt, hailing yet another American triumph on the final drive east.

American tanks fan out across fields near the Rhine River, outflanking the German antitank-gun positions set up to the rear of the burning farmhouses.

Wary of snipers, infantrymen of the U.S. Ninth Army crouch behind an antitank gun at a crossroads in Rheydt, west of Düsseldorf.

A tanker of the 3rd Armored Division machine-guns a nest of German snipers hidden in a wood off the autobahn near Dessau, Germany.

A Sherman tank charges toward an enemy-held ruin in Nuremberg, where diehard Nazis had to be blasted out building by building.

American infantrymen, fording a river
during their advance against German positions
near Waldau, pass a dead SS trooper.

Covering their ears against the noise,
U.S. Third Army mortarmen bombard German
defenders on the east bank of the Rhine.

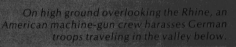
On high ground overlooking the Rhine, an
American machine-gun crew harasses German
troops traveling in the valley below.

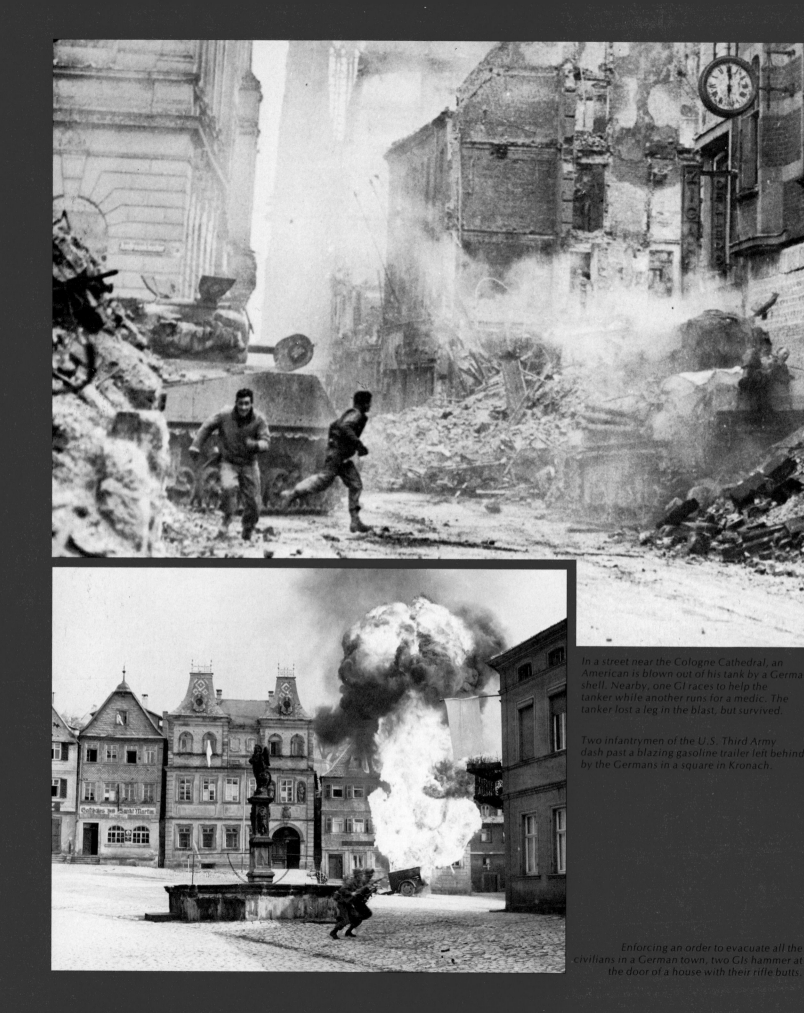

In a street near the Cologne Cathedral, an American is blown out of his tank by a German shell. Nearby, one GI races to help the tanker while another runs for a medic. The tanker lost a leg in the blast, but survived.

Two infantrymen of the U.S. Third Army dash past a blazing gasoline trailer left behind by the Germans in a square in Kronach.

Enforcing an order to evacuate all the civilians in a German town, two GIs hammer at the door of a house with their rifle butts.

Beside the hulk of a self-propelled German 105mm howitzer, GIs inspect a U.S. light tank that had been captured by the Germans.

Driven from their positions by mortar fire, three German soldiers approach the American lines with their hands raised in surrender.

Thousands of German POWs trudge to the rear on the center island of the autobahn near Giessen as U.S. Third Army vehicles head east.

Two exhausted GIs of the 78th Division take a nap in the window of a small-town shop while waiting for orders to advance again.

Battle-weary U.S. First Army troops relax at a shrine in the town of Esch. They had just helped repel a counterattack near Cologne.

FREEING THE CAMPS OF DEATH

Troops of the U.S. 4th Armored Division stare in silent disbelief at the bodies of starved and slaughtered inmates of the Ohrdruf concentration camp.

"LIKE STEPPING INTO THE DARK AGES"

During April 1945, the rapidly advancing Allied armies stumbled on several of the many extermination and concentration camps that the Nazi regime had set up to slaughter Jews and other victims and imprison foreign slave laborers. Even the most battle-hardened soldiers were stunned by what they discovered in the camps.

In the Bergen-Belsen camp British troops found 10,000 unburied corpses. In Dachau the GIs found 33,000 prisoners so emaciated that many of them were too weak to move. Everywhere Allied troops found whips, bludgeons and instruments of torture. Said an American sergeant of his arrival at Nordhausen, where corpses were stacked 75 high: "It was like stepping into the Dark Ages."

The Allied commanders could spare only small forces to help at the camps; the great majority of their doctors, medics and support troops had to press ahead with the combat units. The difficulties notwithstanding, an immediate relief campaign was undertaken. Small task forces scoured the nearby towns and surrounding countryside for emergency rations, called for food and medicines from Army depots in the rear, located German technicians to repair broken water mains and electric-power lines. Prisoners who were strong enough for labor detail helped to scrub down the filthy barracks and to dig new latrines. Inmates with medical training came forward to assist the overworked Army corpsmen. In most of the camps, the prisoners' records had been destroyed by the fleeing SS officers, and each inmate had to fill in lengthy forms to prepare for repatriation at the end of the War.

In the weeks that followed liberation, the prisoners' sickness and malnutrition responded slowly to rest, treatment and a decent diet. But the inmates had suffered deeper damage. "They knock timidly on the doors of our offices, edge fearfully inside and remain rigid even after we tell them to relax," wrote Marcus J. Smith, a medical officer assigned to the Dachau camp. "They have not yet overcome their fear of authority. It will take time for them to become human beings again."

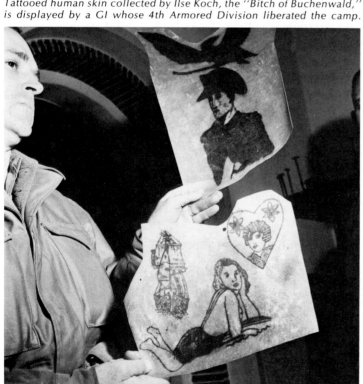

Tattooed human skin collected by Ilse Koch, the "Bitch of Buchenwald," is displayed by a GI whose 4th Armored Division liberated the camp.

Dying of starvation, a prisoner at Bergen-Belsen sits in silent suffering. More than 40,000 slave laborers were discovered there, and thousands of inmates, a British soldier said, "were so weak and listless that they just lay on the ground and took no notice of what was going on, and in fact were difficult to distinguish from the corpses which lay everywhere."

Women prisoners at the Bergen-Belsen camp form a line to receive a dusting of DDT.

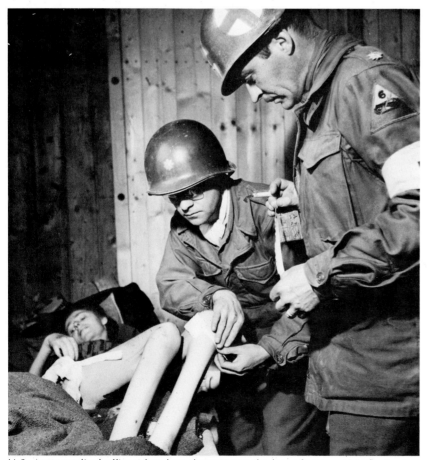

U.S. Army medical officers bandage the sores on the legs of an emaciated prisoner.

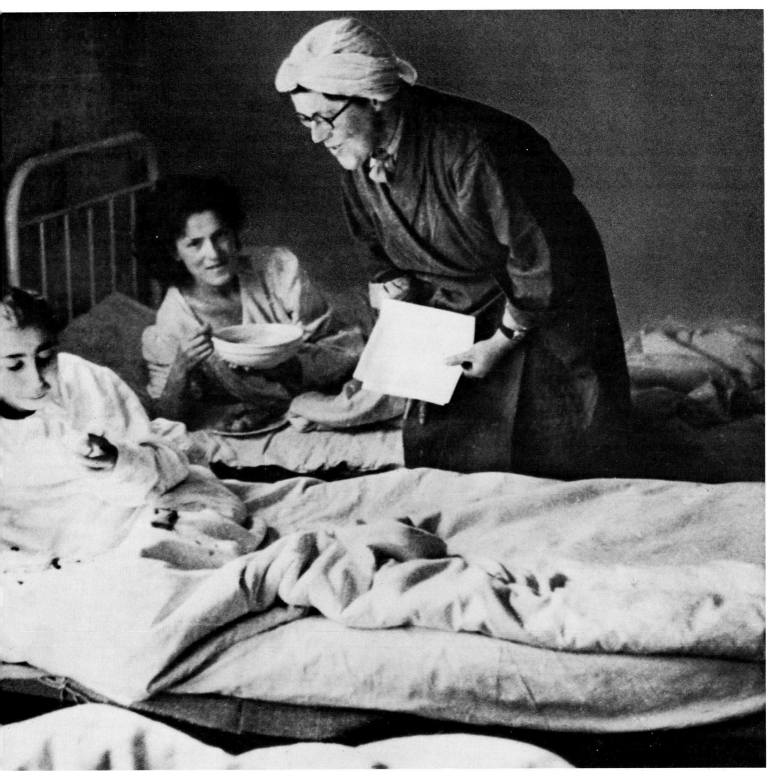

An English volunteer working at Bergen-Belsen for the French Relief Services chats with a group of liberated prisoners at mealtime in a hospital at the camp.

FOOD AND MEDICINE ON THE DOUBLE

Allied task forces hastily went to work to remedy the horrors they discovered in the concentration camps. On the day of liberation at Nordhausen, some 700 inmates were evacuated to makeshift hospitals. Typhus, carried by body lice, was epidemic at several camps; doctors quarantined the compounds and requisitioned great quantities of the new insecticide DDT, which they sprinkled generously over inmates, troops and visitors alike. Vaccinations for typhus followed later.

Food supplies were rushed in. But much of the food was of dubious value. Dachau, for example, quickly received tons of corned beef and ample stocks of sausage—all of which was too rich for prisoners who had subsisted for months and, in some cases, years on scarcely 500 calories a day in the form of thin soup and stale bread. Doctors and medics prevented the inmates from killing themselves by overeating. But hundreds of prisoners perished anyhow, unable to take on enough nourishment to reverse the effects of malnutrition and exhaustion.

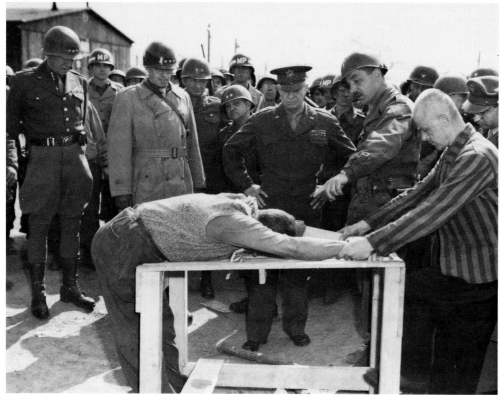

Prisoners reenact SS torture techniques for three generals—from left, Patton, Bradley and Eisenhower.

TELLING THE WORLD THE TERRIBLE TRUTH

General Dwight D. Eisenhower, Supreme Allied Commander, was shaken and enraged by what he saw at Ohrdruf, the first concentration camp to be liberated by the Allies. Rushing to U.S. Third Army headquarters, Ike sent cables to Washington and London, urging that legislators and journalists be brought in to view the horrors of the camp.

From then on, dozens of newsmen and others accompanied the troops into each newly discovered camp. Radio-journalist Edward R. Murrow rode with U.S. Third Army tanks into Buchenwald. Marguerite Higgins, the well-known reporter for the New York *Herald-Tribune*, reached Dachau with the first Allied troops. Pennsylvania Congressman John Kunkel visited Buchenwald; when reporters asked his opinion, he said grimly: "If you tried to tell the actual facts, you'd get into filth and obscenity that would be unprintable."

The Allied commanders ordered townspeople from adjacent communities to inspect the camps. The local citizens were spared nothing. They saw the stacks of corpses, the gallows, the ovens in which the dead were cremated.

Nearly all of the Germans were sickened, and a few were profoundly affected. After a tour of the Ohrdruf camp, the mayor of the town and his wife hanged themselves. Some Germans admitted that they had realized terrible things were going on in the camps, but insisted that they had been powerless to do anything about it.

Still others, however, said that they had known nothing of the atrocities—a view derided by a correspondent for *Yank* magazine. Many of the prisoners, he wrote, had, after all, been in plain sight. "They collapsed of hunger at their benches and no one asked why. They died along the road on the long walk back to camp and no one expressed surprise. The good citizens shut their eyes and their ears and their nostrils to the sight and sound and the smell of this place."

German townspeople stand shocked and weeping

...uring a tour of the Buchenwald camp. They had seen a truck loaded with corpses, and an American officer had described the SS atrocities committed there.

Assembling for a burial detail, 1,000 citizens of Gardelegen shoulder wooden crosses symbolizing the martyrdom of camp inmates murdered by the SS.

FOR THE VICTIMS, A DECENT BURIAL

Who would bury the dead prisoners?

The Allied commanders were bent on teaching the German people an object lesson. On their orders, citizens of nearby towns, along with the captured Germans who had run the camps, were required to load the bodies into trucks and horse-drawn wagons and carry them to burial grounds deliberately chosen in prominent places to remind the Germans of the atrocities. There, at last, the victims received a funeral service and a decent burial.

At General Eisenhower's direction a fitting memorial was planned for the German citizens at the town of Gardelegen, where no fewer than 1,000 political pris-oners had been locked in a barn drenched with gasoline and had been burned to death. One thousand townspeople were chosen, each person to bury one prisoner in a special cemetery in the municipal park. Every German was responsible, from that time onward, for tending the grave—and to remind each one of the townspeople of his duty, his name as well as that of the victim was inscribed on the headstone.

166

An SS sergeant major at Bergen-Belsen carries a victim to a burial site.

Bergen-Belsen guards fill a mass grave with the bodies of inmates.

A recently liberated prisoner at Buchenwald confronts and accuses one of his former captors.

Standing over a camp guard, two Dachau inmates pelt him with insults and recrimination.

THE PRISONERS' REVENGE

At every camp, the freed prisoners took revenge on their former captors, and the Allies were in no hurry to stop them. Most inmates were content to curse and spit at their tormentors. Others gathered evidence for war-crimes trials. In some cases the prisoners demanded immediate retribution. "Almost daily, SS men are flushed out of hiding places," wrote a medical officer at Dachau. "Yesterday one was discovered and impaled on the front gate."

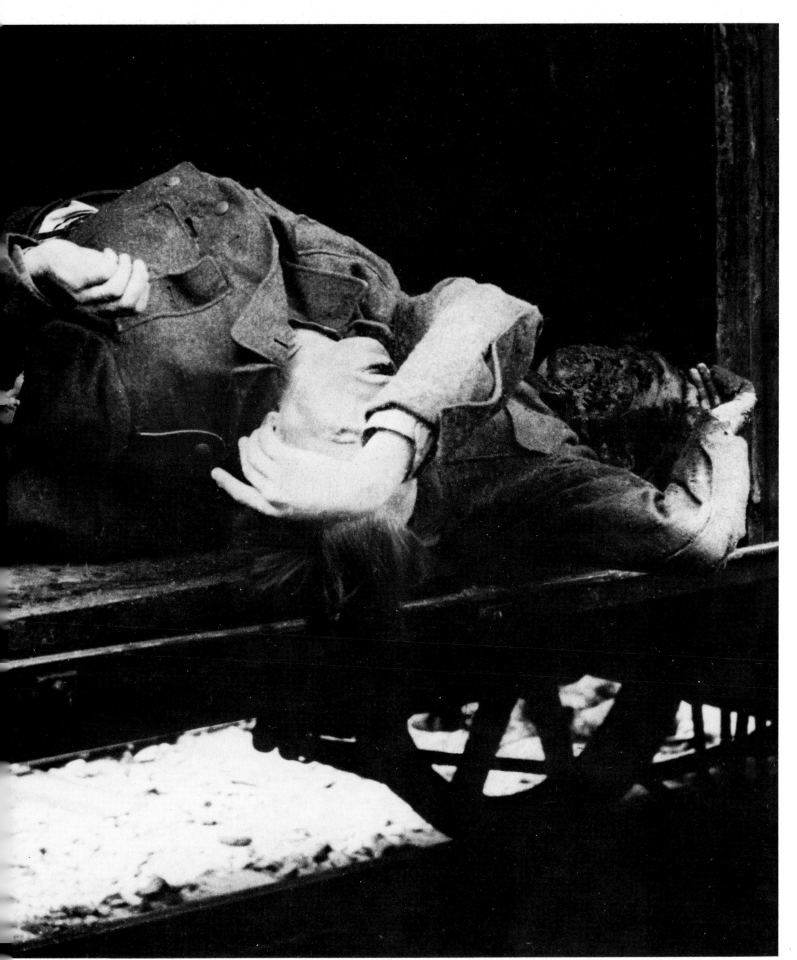

Victims of the prisoners' vengeance, two SS troopers sprawl in a railway wagon near the Dachau camp, where they had been seized and killed by prisoners.

5

Every farm boy in GI uniform knew the old saying about snakes with broken backs: Their tails were supposed to twitch until sunset before they died. That was the condition of the Wehrmacht in April 1945. Everywhere, the GIs were advancing almost at will against broken divisions, corps and armies. Every day, Germans surrendered in droves. An infantry officer said, "If you fire your pistol in the air, a dozen Germans will come rushing in to be taken prisoner." And yet other Germans did fight and fight hard.

Typically, these last twitches were brief, vicious clashes along country roads between towns with soon-forgotten names. "You thrust past huge roadblocks where the Germans had hastily improvised defenses," reported Time-Life correspondent Sidney Olson, following an armored unit on its drive eastward. "Around these lie the old familiar signs of another lost German battle, the scattered helmets, the ripped-off pants legs and coat arms where wounds were dressed, the golden sprinkles of ammunition, the smashed machine guns and the still-smouldering trucks overturned in the ditches. After the armor had broken through this last crust, it had merely taken off in great wide swoops over all the great road network." And miles later, "you come to debris of war again, a bend in the road where the fleeing Germans turned for a delaying action. You can see the tank tracks where the tankers hurriedly tore out into the fields to hit the Germans from several sides at once. The smashed trucks, guns and equipment are scattered colorfully over the fields, the scene much like a littered picnic ground where the picnickers will never yawn awake again."

The worst of it for the GIs was that they never could guess when the enemy would vanish, or when he would fight. They never knew what awaited them around the next bend in the road—a surrender or an ambush. The GIs had no intention of dying in a war already won, and they could not understand why some Germans were willing to die for a cause already lost, especially since each fight tore up their farms or brought down ruin on their towns. Why were the Germans still fighting on? How long would it take for the Wehrmacht's tail to stop twitching?

Under the plan set forth by General Eisenhower, the destruction of the German forces trapped inside the Ruhr pocket was merely the centerpiece of a gigantic Allied of-

PURSUIT TO THE ELBE

fensive all along the Western Front. As elements of the U.S. First and Ninth Armies crushed Field Marshal Model's hapless troops, the main bodies of those armies were sweeping east to the Elbe River and its principal tributary, the Mulde.

At the same time, the rest of the Allied armies were driving forward in many directions. In Holland, troops of the Canadian First Army pushed north toward Arnhem and northeast toward the estuary of the Weser River and the German naval base at Wilhelmshaven. Below the Canadians, the British Second Army headed east toward the Elbe and northeast toward the great North Sea ports of Bremen and Hamburg. In the south, below the Ruhr, the U.S. Third Army was slanting southeast toward the city of Chemnitz, scarcely 20 miles from the border of Czechoslovakia. To the right of the Third Army, the two armies of the U.S. Sixth Army Group pushed into southern Germany. The U.S. Seventh Army attacked toward the Austrian border. The French First Army drove southward into the Black Forest, intent on settling scores with the hated Boches before the War ended. Without any question, the western half of Germany would soon be sliced to ribbons by Allied forces in hot pursuit of shattered Wehrmacht units.

Eisenhower's primary objective, the Elbe River, was an important one. Nearly all of Germany's surviving industry was concentrated along the Elbe in the cities of Dresden, Wittenberge, Torgau, Dessau and Magdeburg. The river was navigable for 525 miles on its way from Czechoslovakia to the North Sea, and big boats could bring supplies to within 50 miles of Berlin. The Elbe was also a wide river— wide enough to make a safe and natural restraining line for the converging forces of the Allies and the Soviet Union.

For reasons known only to himself, Eisenhower had not yet informed his Army commanders of his decision to abandon Berlin as the Allies' final objective. Possibly the Supreme Commander was withholding this information because it was bound to disappoint the men and might impair their performance in the drive. Bradley, one of Eisenhower's few confidants, revealed nothing of the decision; in early April, Bradley's orders to Patton's Third Army and Hodges' First Army still called for crossing the Elbe, which suggested an attack on Berlin. Bradley went even further in his orders for Simpson's Ninth Army, which Montgomery had returned to Bradley's command on April 4. The Ninth Army

was to "exploit any opportunity for seizing a bridgehead over the Elbe and be prepared to advance on Berlin or to the northeast."

Simpson immediately announced his army's assignment, and when the troops heard the magic word "Berlin," they gleefully assumed that they had been specially chosen to capture the German capital. "My people were keyed up," Simpson recalled. "We'd been the first to the Rhine and now we were going to be the first to Berlin. All along we thought of just one thing—capturing Berlin, going through and meeting the Russians on the other side."

On April 4, the Ninth and First Armies had paused to regroup after the opening phase of the Ruhr assault. The Ninth's 2nd Armored Division and the First's 3rd Armored Division, which had snapped the trap shut around the Ruhr, moved into position to lead the drive east. Then, with these divisions slashing open a wide path, the armies renewed their offensive. Overwhelming tactical air support did the rest. In several areas, the front-running tanks burst into the clear, and the Germans reeled backward.

In the first days of April, realistic German generals took it for granted that their tattered, tank-poor forces could not fight a war of maneuver against Bradley's swift and massive thrust into the midsection of the Reich, presumably aimed at Berlin. They would have to defend fixed positions and every obstructive terrain feature—forests, rugged uplands and the numerous streams flowing south to north in the Americans' path. When each stand had held up the advance as long as possible, the surviving defenders would have to scramble back to the next defensible point, and there buy still more time for new German divisions to be scraped together. This sort of catch-as-catch-can fighting was highly un-German, and it also violated Hitler's orders to hold at all cost. Field Marshal Albert Kesselring, the Commander in Chief West, disgustedly called it "the makeshift campaign."

Adolf Hitler in his Berlin headquarters still thought that some miracle would save the Reich. On the night of April 1, he had issued a universal call to arms over the Greater German Radio network. All men, women and children, the radio directive ordered, were to form underground organizations and launch a guerrilla campaign of sabotage and terrorism behind the Allied lines. The new army of fighters would be known as Werewolves. The call to arms met with a lackluster response. But here and there groups of thoroughly Nazified youngsters proved themselves willing to die for their Führer—"as if," a German general later said sarcastically, "what the Wehrmacht had failed to do could be accomplished by a rabble of Boy Scouts."

Hitler had followed up on April 2 with an order that all towns and cities be defended to the death. To enforce this edict, local Nazi leaders were appointed "combat commanders" and given absolute control over all military, paramilitary and civilian personnel in their towns or cities. But this order proved as difficult to implement as the ill-fated Werewolf campaign. "The defense of a town," explained Kesselring, "demanded a high degree of tactical experience, training and combat discipline as well as suitable terrain that could not be outflanked." Only a handful of the towns and cities were favorably situated, and the defense forces available to most combat commanders were a sorry collection of *Volkssturm,* local police and stragglers from Army and Air Force units.

The Führer next addressed himself to the critical problem of large-scale surrenders, desertions and defeatism in the ranks. He issued orders to all units warning that even talk of surrender was punishable by summary execution.

Certain SS commanders made liberal use of the order. In the Main River town of Lohr, in the U.S. Seventh Army's zone, SS troops hanged six prominent citizens who had shown too little enthusiasm for defending the town. When the Americans besieged the nearby town of Aschaffenburg, SS men machine-gunned citizens who tried to escape. On entering the town, infantrymen of the U.S. 45th Division found a German lieutenant dangling from a steel overhang in front of a wine shop with his executioners' warning pinned to his clothing: "Cowards and traitors hang! Yesterday, an officer candidate died a hero's death destroying an enemy tank. He lives on! Today, a coward in officer's garb hangs because he betrayed the Führer and the people. He is dead forever!"

Most Wehrmacht senior officers shunned such barbaric measures, but agreed with the sentiments behind them. Kesselring believed that patriotism and honor were absolutes, that a man should fight to the death if so ordered and never mind whether the war was lost. He admired the bravery of men who perished in suicidal stands—"the primitive duty of comradeship," he called it. He despaired to think that the performance of a unit depended not on loyalty but on "the good will of officers and men—morale in other words."

On April 6, Hitler turned his attention to purely military affairs and instituted a wholesale realignment of commands in an effort to halt the Allied drive. The old order of battle, with Army Groups B, H and G under the command of Kesselring, no longer made sense. Field Marshal Model's Army Group B was surrounded and was fighting for its life in the Ruhr, and General Blaskowitz' Army Group H was now threatened with isolation in the north by the British and Canadians. Army Group G had been driven back by the U.S. Third Army's swift attacks on the southern Rhine.

Accordingly, Hitler split the Western Front in two, with the east-west dividing line running just to the south of Brunswick and Magdeburg. North of this boundary, the former Army Group H was redesignated OB (German Armed Forces) Northwest and placed under Field Marshal Ernst Busch, a veteran of the Russian front and recently the commander of the German north-coast defenses. Kesselring's reduced command, OB West, now consisted of four badly mauled armies. The strongest of the weak lot were the First and Nineteenth Armies in the zone of the U.S. Sixth Army Group. Kesselring's Seventh Army, which faced the U.S. Third Army, was feeble at best; its broken units were raiding Luftwaffe and SS installations and civilian warehouses for food and, for fuel, were confiscating the hoarded gasoline supplies of local Nazi Party officials. The troops bitterly nicknamed these caches "flight fuel."

The weakest army in Kesselring's command was the Eleventh. It was put together from units that had been smashed by U.S. armor east of the Ruhr and driven back to the vulnerable northern sector of Kesselring's front, facing the U.S. First Army. The Eleventh was so weak that Kesselring on April 8 ordered it to withdraw into defensive positions in the Harz Mountains, leaving some units to guard the western approach to the Harz along the Leine River.

On the northern front, Field Marshal Busch found himself in charge of the Twenty-fifth Army in the Netherlands, one corps of the scattered First Parachute Army, in northwestern Germany, and a hastily organized force charged with defending a line that ran all the way from the central front to the north coast. In addition, Busch was given command of all German Navy and Luftwaffe forces in his zone—a highly irregular procedure that underscored the desperate shortage of manpower in the Army.

Hitler also juggled Busch's subordinate commanders. He transferred General Blaskowitz, formerly the commander of Army Group H, to the top post in Holland. He relieved the commander of the First Parachute Army, General Günther Blumentritt, and replaced him with one of his favorites, the aggressive, hard-driving General Kurt Student, who had won renown as the commander of the forces that had captured Crete in 1941.

The personnel changes could hardly make up for the dire shortages of men and matériel, but at a staff meeting Hitler waxed eloquent over the dramatic improvements he expected from Student's appointment. General Alfred Jodl, the Führer's obsequious chief of operations staff, summoned the nerve to tell Hitler the truth: "You may send up a dozen Students, *mein Führer,* but it won't alter the situation."

To complete his new arrangements, the Führer produced one of his allegedly miraculous plans. He would turn the tide with the Twelfth Army. This formation, which he had officially activated on April 2, was being pieced together

with remnants and reserves of all sorts: trainees at panzer and engineer schools, cadets from officer-training academies, convalescents from Berlin hospitals, conscripts from a paramilitary labor force. While this army assembled on the east bank of the Elbe, it would be protected by the Eleventh Army's defense in the Harz Mountains to the west. Then, under the leadership of some of Germany's best and brightest officers, the Twelfth Army would push all the way from the Elbe to the Rhine, relieving Model's trapped forces in the Ruhr and simultaneously driving a wedge between Montgomery's and Bradley's armies.

On April 6, Hitler found the right leader for his new army. He was 45-year-old Walter Wenck, one of the youngest generals in the Wehrmacht. Wenck had distinguished himself as a staff officer in France and as an army-group chief of staff in the Soviet Union; he then was promoted to the post of director of operations and deputy chief of staff at Army High Command headquarters in East Prussia. There, Wenck had first attracted the Führer's attention with a plain-spoken report on conditions in the Soviet Union: "As you see, my Führer, the whole of the Eastern Front is like a Swiss cheese—full of holes." Though Wenck was reprimanded for using such informal language, Hitler commended the "liveliness" of his report.

Wenck was also known as a prankster. In France he had once ordered an antiaircraft gun fired outside his hotel headquarters, the object being to scare a visiting general out of his bathtub. The general rushed out, dripping wet and half-naked, to be greeted by uproarious laughter. In the Soviet Union, Wenck had raised the eyebrows of colleagues by sending orders and queries in rhymed quatrains.

Wenck was in Bavaria recuperating from a serious automobile accident on the Russian front when he received a call from Hitler's chief of Army personnel, General Wilhelm Burgdorf, on April 6. Burgdorf announced, "The Führer has named you commander of the Twelfth Army."

"The Twelfth Army?" Wenck said. "I've never heard of a Twelfth Army."

"The Twelfth Army," General Burgdorf snapped, "is being organized now."

Wenck pulled his uniform over the surgical corset that protected his crushed ribs and prepared to head north to Berlin to find out more about his peculiar new assignment.

A pair of GIs cut the wire bonds from the body of a German soldier who had been hanged, along with 10 others, for advocating the surrender of Schweinfurt in central Germany. Many such executions were ordered as object lessons by local commanders, who themselves were threatened with death if their forces failed to fight to the last man.

Bradley's three armies made uneven early progress during the new phase of the offensive. Patton's Third Army took several towns on April 4. One, Kassel, fell to the 80th Infantry Division after a fierce fight. But a combat command of the spearhead 4th Armored Division took Gotha without any fight whatsoever; the garrison troops were found in a hospital disguised as patients.

Another combat command of the 4th Armored took the nearby town of Ohrdruf, and there the tankers were horrified to find the first of many concentration camps, whose existence was as yet nearly unknown in the Allied world. The hellhole was crowded with starving slave laborers; unburied corpses lay everywhere. When General Patton came to see the appalling scene, he vomited.

Soon Patton's northern forces were slowed up by a series of small-scale counterattacks by the rear-guard units of Kesselring's retreating Eleventh Army. It was not until April 10 that the Third Army was able to make good headway again.

To the north of Patton, Hodges' First Army got off to a slow start on April 5, and immediately it was held up by fierce resistance from the same SS panzer training units that had caused so much trouble early in the Ruhr assault. After beating off the SS troopers, First Army units arrived at the Weser River on April 6, only to find that all of the bridges had been blown. During the next few days two infantry divisions, the 2nd and the 69th, crossed over and took the university town of Göttingen without a fight. The two divisions then crossed the Leine River and pushed on toward their Leipzig objective.

To the north of the First Army, Simpson's Ninth Army made rapid progress in its advance toward Magdeburg on the Elbe, just 79 miles short of Berlin. On April 5 the Ninth's spearhead, General Isaac D. White's tough 2nd Armored Division, reached Hameln, the town made famous by the Pied Piper legend. Hameln was a pretty little place—but not for long. It was strongly defended by an SS unit, and the Americans were forced to flatten it. Beyond Hameln, the 2nd Armored reached open, rolling country that stretched away 100-odd miles to the Elbe.

Now the tankers encountered little resistance. The remnants of the First Parachute Army retreated to the north, and the tankers pushed aside weak units left behind by the Eleventh Army to cover its retreat into the Harz Mountains. A

combat command captured Hildesheim on April 7, and by then the 2nd Armored was so far ahead of the First and Third Armies that General Simpson called a halt on April 7 to give the others time to catch up and draw abreast.

Behind and to the north of the 2nd Armored, the 84th Infantry Division attacked Hanover, the biggest city on the Ninth Army's route to the Elbe. The thin German defenses posed no serious problem, especially after some GIs captured a map showing that most of the enemy strength was stacked to the south and southeast of the city. Hanover fell on April 10.

Behind the 2nd Armored and to its south, the 83rd Division was moving almost as fast as the tankers, and one of its regiments was making an unlikely spectacle of itself. The regiment's proper designation was the 329th Infantry, but a nickname coined for it by a newspaperman fairly well described its unorthodox appearance: the Ragtag Circus.

This outfit, commanded with dash by Colonel Edwin B. "Buckshot" Crabill, suffered from a disability that afflicted every standard infantry regiment. Its service company had just enough trucks to transport one of its three battalions at a time. To pick up speed, Crabill's men had commandeered everything on wheels that they could lay their hands on as they advanced: German trucks, municipal fire engines, horse-drawn wagons, even cement mixers. The GIs especially favored German buses, which could carry 50 men

In a gripping sequence of photographs taken by Robert Capa on the 18th of April, 1945, just before the surrender of Leipzig, a young U.S. corporal helps a buddy fire a machine gun from a balcony to protect Americans crossing a bridge below. Suddenly, the corporal slumps and falls back into the apartment, slain by a sniper's bullet. A sergeant takes over the machine gun, and the Germans defending the bridge are soon routed. "The last day some of the best ones die," said Capa.

with tolerable overcrowding. And so, with its scouts speeding ahead on bicycles—two GIs to a bike—the 329th was, at the very least, a ragtag circus.

The Ragtag Circus was not far behind when the 2nd Armored resumed its drive on April 10. The tankers rolled forward in a four-column attack formation, with a reconnaissance company in the van of each column and tanks and half-tracks following behind. The Ragtag Circus and its parent 83rd Division, along with the 30th Division, moved parallel to the 2nd Armored's main body, mopping up pockets of resistance.

The makeshift German forces in the Brunswick area did the best they could to stop the tanks, cranking down their big 88mm antiaircraft guns and using them as antitank weapons. The 2nd Armored's Combat Command A ran into the flak belt defending the Hermann Göring Steelworks near the town of Immendorf, just southwest of Brunswick. The tankers quickly spread out and outflanked the gun positions. By the time the steelworks fell at 8 p.m. on April 10, they had knocked out 67 heavy enemy guns.

To the south the 2nd Armored's Combat Command B column, led by Brigadier General Sidney R. Hinds, tangled with eight more of the 88mm guns at a strong roadblock just east of Salzgitter late on April 10. Outflanking the guns, Hinds's men quickly cleared the roadblock and seized a bridge over the Oker River, about 46 miles from the Elbe.

The next day, April 11, the 2nd Armored burned up the road. Hinds's command raced out of its little bridgehead and roared ahead full throttle, bowling over small roadblocks. At one point the tankers encountered a 1,700-man German column marching along the road, searching for someone to accept their surrender. Leaving a guard detail behind to secure the prisoners, Hinds's column rolled on.

After dark on April 11 a column of Hinds's tanks, commanded by Major James F. Hollingsworth, reached Schönebeck, seven miles south of Magdeburg on the Elbe. The tankers spotted a bridge up ahead and made a dash for it. The lead tanks rumbled to within 40 feet of the bridge, but were driven back by intense German fire. Before a new attack with infantry could reach the bridge, the Germans blew it up in Hollingsworth's face.

It was a bitter disappointment for the tankers. But there was jubilation at Ninth Army headquarters when, shortly after 8 p.m. on April 11, an electrifying message arrived from 2nd Armored headquarters: "We're on the Elbe."

The 2nd Armored had covered 73 miles in one day to gain the river. The 83rd Infantry Division was not far behind. The Ragtag Circus had logged 32 miles on April 11, and late on April 12 it had reached the Elbe at the town of Barby, a few miles upstream from Schönebeck.

The same day, 50 miles downstream from Magdeburg at Tangermünde, the Ninth Army's 5th Armored Division also

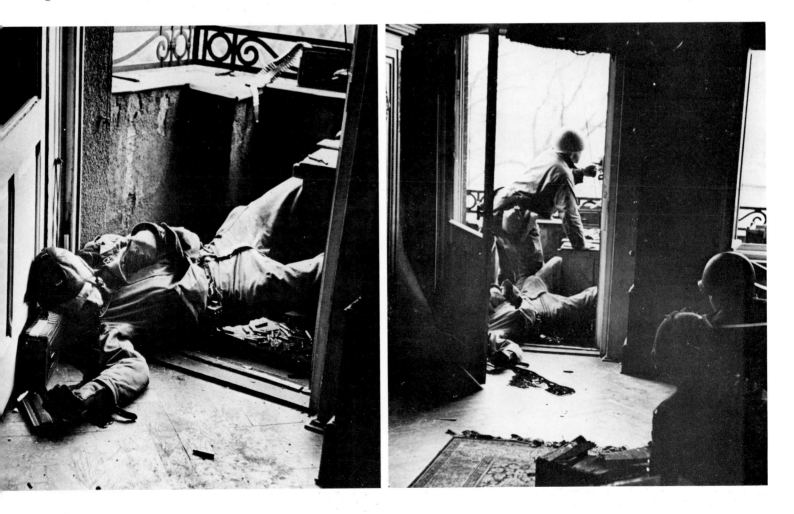

175

reached the Elbe, at a point only 53 miles from Berlin. The Ninth Army was now on the Elbe in strength, and the troops still thought they were going to Berlin.

In the dash to the Elbe, the Ninth Army units had passed to the north of the Harz Mountains, a block of rugged peaks running northwest-southeast for 60 miles to a maximum width of 20 miles. According to Hitler's plan, the Eleventh Army was supposed to retreat into the Harz and delay the Americans so that General Wenck would have time to marshal his Twelfth Army east of the Elbe. Neither Field Marshal Kesselring nor Lieut. General Walther Lucht, commanding the Eleventh Army, had seen much point in Hitler's plan for the Harz, and the plan became absolutely pointless as the Ninth Army outflanked the mountains to the north. Nevertheless, Lucht had no real choice in the matter; his chewed-up forces had failed to hold back the onrushing tanks of the U.S. First Army on the flat Thuringian plain, and he had to retreat to some defensible position. There was nowhere to go but the Harz Mountains.

Duty-bound to the core, Lucht sacrificed one of his three depleted corps in an attempt to delay the U.S. First Army and to hold open a corridor between the Harz and the town of Halle, so that Wenck's much-bruited army could attack westward through the oncoming Americans. Then with his two remaining corps, Lucht headed into the mountains.

General Lucht's considered opinion of his rear-guard action was blunt and succinct: a ''hopeless mission.'' His command—roughly 70,000 men—was the usual jumble of weary Wehrmacht men, SS troopers, local policemen and training-school youths. It even included some stragglers from a unit of ulcer victims, the 281st Stomach Ailment Battalion, one of several such units formed to simplify the treatment of soldiers suffering from the same kind of illness. Moreover, there was a critical shortage of weapons and supplies, and no time to build decent defensive positions. But Lucht was an officer of the old school; he shrugged off his intimations of disaster and prepared his troops for a fight.

Large numbers of small units fanned out through the Harz. Some occupied the forests of pine and fir that clung to the lower slopes. Others moved into the crags above the winding roads that connected a sprinkling of picturesque mountain towns, and there set up artillery positions.

Lucht's struggle began on April 11. His troops were attacked by units of two First Army infantry divisions, the 1st coming from the west, and the 104th striking from the south. Lucht's units used guerrilla tactics that infuriated the GIs of the 1st Division. They would let the Americans push them back through the gorges and defiles, and then, just when their defeat and capture seemed imminent, they would disappear into the wooded hills beyond. Frequently the Germans would double back and attack their pursuers from behind, inflicting casualties before vanishing once again. For a time, neither side gained an appreciable edge in this skirmishing.

Soon, however, the First Army troops got help from the main body of the Ninth Army, then passing to the north. A regiment of the 83rd Division—a brother outfit of the Ragtag Circus—and a combat command of the 8th Armored Division stabbed into the Harz's northern fringes. At the same time the First Army's 9th Division swept in from the east and south. The Germans could not hold the GIs back.

Facing a stern-faced bust of the immortal Johann Sebastian Bach, a GI sits at the keyboard of a harpsichord once played by the composer himself. The instrument was discovered by soldiers of the U.S. Third Army in Bach's home in the town of Eisenach.

On April 14, the German stand took a fateful turn; troops of the 1st and 83rd Divisions linked up in the Harz interior. Now Lucht's command was cut in two, with both halves surrounded and running out of room. As the Americans closed in on all sides, Lucht had to move his command post from the town of Braunlage to a nearby limestone quarry. In the next few days, he had to move four times more—to a forester's cottage, a cave, a monastery and a wooded slope near Blankenburg, a town on the eastern edge of the Harz mountain range.

The Americans were everywhere. They captured one village after another and sealed off the roads to the Germans. The 1st Division's haul of prisoners rose from about 200 to 1,000 daily. The 1st's gunners knocked out four German tanks on April 15 and 10 more on the 17th. By then Lucht's pitiful army had only a few tanks left.

All through the first week of fighting, a group of about 200 Germans had held the 3,747-foot-high Brocken, the highest peak in the Harz range. But on April 18 they were attacked by forces they could not withstand. Fighter-bombers of the IX Tactical Air Command, flying with fuel pods attached to their wings for extra range, plastered the German positions on the lofty crag. The next day American infantry stormed the peak and overwhelmed the German survivors.

Lucht and his senior officers realized that they could accomplish nothing by holding out any longer; the infantry attacks from both north and south had long since proved that they had been outflanked by the armored spearheads of the U.S. Ninth and First Armies. Scattered German commanders began attempts to negotiate a surrender.

The Americans, eager to end the battle without more casualties, gladly obliged. On April 20, Colonel Edwin Burba, at the head of a combat command of the 8th Armored, pulled up on the outskirts of Blankenburg to offer the German commander there a chance to surrender. A meeting was arranged, and Burba made his proposal. The German declined to surrender on the grounds of duty, but he did so in a manner that invited some sort of face-saving device. Burba obligingly suggested that an overwhelming show of U.S. force might make a convincing argument for surrender. The German agreed that a token attack by 100 U.S. tanks would permit him to capitulate with honor.

Burba did not have 100 tanks, but would 50 do? The German replied that 50 tanks sounded intimidating. So 50 U.S. tanks made a mock attack and were met with mock resistance, after which the surrender took place. All night long, Germans emerged from buildings and strong points in the town, asking directions to the nearest prisoner-of-war cage.

One by one, the remaining pockets of German resistance gave up the struggle. Lucht himself finally surrendered on April 23 to an 8th Armored Division captain. Lucht remarked with pride that he was the last Eleventh Army general to be captured, and that, he said, was "as it should be."

Actually, for all its stubborn valor, the stand of Lucht's command could never have served its purpose. The Americans could easily have bypassed the Harz and let Lucht's troops wither on the vine; the U.S. commanders attacked only because they had manpower to spare. But while Lucht had failed to protect General Wenck's nascent Twelfth Army, that pickup force had already done astonishingly well without any help whatsoever.

After General Wenck had learned of his new assignment on April 6, he concluded that it would be the death of him, and he prepared accordingly. He bade his wife, Irmgard, farewell and told her to stay in the Bavarian Alps come what may; it was the safest place in the crumbling Reich. Then he detoured to Weimar hoping to withdraw his life's savings—some 10,000 reichsmarks—from his bank. To Wenck's amazement and chagrin, that city had already fallen to troops of Patton's Third Army. So he headed for his Twelfth Army headquarters, 62 miles southwest of Berlin and 57 miles east of the Harz Mountains. Travel was very difficult. The roads were choked with fleeing soldiers and civilians, some hurrying east to escape the onrushing Americans and others rushing west to escape the advancing Russians.

On April 12, Wenck finally reached his command post at Rosslau, near Dessau. It was housed comfortably in a Wehrmacht training school overlooking the Elbe, but what he saw there dismayed him. Though he had been promised about 100,000 men, he had scarcely half that many and barely a dozen tanks. The troops were a miscellaneous lot whose chief assets seemed to be their youthful eagerness and a series of heroic unit names, such as Division Clausewitz, Division Scharnhorst and Division Ulrich von Hutten.

Wenck immediately put aside all thoughts of the Führer's

wild plan for a Twelfth Army drive to rescue the armies trapped in the Ruhr. His situation maps showed an impossible predicament. His skimpy army was responsible for an enormous front 125 miles long, stretching along the Elbe and the Mulde from Wittenberge in the north to Leipzig in the south. Since Wenck could hardly defend any point on the line if he spread his forces out all along it, he commandeered some vehicles and divided a large part of his army into mobile shock units that could speed to any threatened position. If the plan worked, and if his stock of gasoline lasted, he might hold the line until the rest of the promised troops could be mustered.

Wenck had learned on his arrival that the U.S. Ninth Army had reached the Elbe in two places, and he set out to do something about it. The greater threat was posed by the crack 2nd Armored Division, which was drawing up on the west bank at Westerhüsen. On the night of April 12, the 2nd Armored pushed two battalions across the river by boat and established a bridgehead just south of Magdeburg. Acting on his mobile-defense plan, Wenck withdrew the defense force in Magdeburg, bolstered it with some home-guard units and started preparing for a counterattack.

To make an attack even more urgent and more difficult, the Americans ferried a third battalion across the Elbe before daylight on April 13. Meanwhile, the 2nd Armored's engineers worked feverishly to bridge the river with pontoons and treadway tracks. With the bridge in place, the 2nd Armored could send across tanks and antitank guns to hold the bridgehead. Without the bridge, the three battalions, which had been rushed across with nothing bigger than machine guns and bazookas, might be overrun.

Through all of the bridge building, German 88mm gun crews in Magdeburg sent high-velocity shells screaming in on the engineers. But the Americans seemed to lead a charmed life. With shells bursting all around them, they worked past dawn and all morning, extending the bridge to within 25 yards of the far shore. Then, around noon on the 13th, a deluge of shells wrecked the whole construction.

Thereupon, the commander of the 2nd Armored, General White, gave up the bridging effort near Magdeburg and radioed orders for his units on the far shore to break out of their bridgehead after dark and establish another bridgehead three miles upstream at the destroyed Schönebeck bridge, out of range of the Magdeburg 88s.

That night the east-bank battalions moved out of their bridgehead and started working their way south. For a time, they seemed to be doing well. Near dawn on April 14, two units were in the town of Elbenau, a few miles southeast of Magdeburg, and one battalion had cleared 250 Germans out of a nearby riverside village. Other small units were digging in on open ground to form a defense perimeter.

Just before daybreak, General Wenck was finally able to launch his counterattack. A regiment of Division Scharnhorst, supported by eight armored vehicles and assault guns, quickly broke through the defense line at the new bridgehead. The Americans traded volleys with the German infantrymen, but the fire fight soon became a rout. About 20 GIs surrendered. The Germans forced them to walk in front of their tanks as they moved on to attack the ring of American defenders. Behind this human shield, the Germans went from foxhole to foxhole, around the perimeter, killing or capturing about 20 men at point-blank range.

The Americans desperately called in artillery on their own positions. The shells broke up the German attack, but

Teams of Army engineers lay down a stretch of runway for an American air base in Germany. Paved runways were too time-consuming to build, so the engineers used prefabricated steel mats, which could be connected together to form a finished airstrip in 24 hours.

the bridgehead was doomed. By 11 a.m. one battalion of GIs had lost its effectiveness as a fighting unit. The 2nd Armored radioed its corps headquarters for air support, but none was available; airstrips had not been moved forward quickly enough to keep pace with the armor, and the Elbe was just beyond the range of fighter planes—even those with fuel pods attached. So at 1:30 p.m. General Hinds, in overall command from the west bank, grimly gave the order for the beleaguered GIs to withdraw back across the Elbe as best they could.

By late afternoon on April 14 most of the survivors had got back safely to the west bank by small boat. Throughout the night and the next day, other survivors trickled in. The casualties in the three battalions totaled 330 dead, wounded, missing or taken prisoner. It was a bitter blow for the proud tankers. For the first time in 30 months of combat in Europe, the 2nd Armored Division had been thrown back.

General Wenck did not settle for that one surprising victory. For six days his army's Division Clausewitz—actually a skeletal task force of scarcely 600 men and 33 assorted armored vehicles—raided the Ninth Army's northern flank, harassing communications and supply lines. On April 14, Wenck even sent Division Clausewitz on an attempt to break through to General Lucht's diehard forces in the Harz Mountains. But that foray proved to be overambitious. Division Clausewitz was trapped by two American infantry regiments and a combat command of the 5th Armored Division. In an effort to escape back to the Elbe, the German commander broke up his force into small groups, most of which were captured.

Two other Twelfth Army divisions, the Scharnhorst and the Ulrich von Hutten, caused the Americans more than a little trouble. At Halle and Dessau in mid-April, they put up a stiff fight against the VII Corps of the First Army. But Wenck was forced to give up his battle against the Americans. The threat of a Russian attack between him and Berlin prompted him to move his forces to an area northeast of Magdeburg. There his Twelfth Army took up positions facing the oncoming Soviet armies.

On April 15, while the Ninth Army was still consoling itself over the 2nd Armored Division's casualties at the Westerhüsen bridgehead, General Simpson got a call from Bradley.

"I've got something very important to tell you," Bradley said, "and I don't want to say it on the phone."

Simpson, armed with a plan for his army's attack toward Berlin, flew to Wiesbaden in a light plane, and Bradley met him at the airfield. He had shocking news.

"You must stop on the Elbe," Bradley said. "You are not to advance any farther in the direction of Berlin. I'm sorry, Simp, but there it is."

Stunned, Simpson blurted out, "Where in the hell did you get this?"

"From Ike," Bradley replied.

Simpson returned disconsolate to the Elbe. At the 2nd Armored Division headquarters on the Elbe, he met General Hinds and told him, "Keep some of your men on the east bank if you want to. But they're not to go any farther."

Incredulous, Hinds was sure there was some mistake. "No, sir," he said. "That's not right. We're going to Berlin."

Following an uncomfortable pause, Simpson replied in a monotone, "We're not going to Berlin, Sid. This is the end of the War for us."

And it was—not just for the Ninth Army but also for Gen-

American soldiers look over the gleaming fuselages of partially completed Heinkel-162 jet fighters, discovered on an assembly line 984 feet below the surface in a salt mine near Engels. Heavy Allied bombing had forced the Germans to move their jet production to subterranean factories built by slave laborers under SS guard; at its peak, this plant produced between 40 and 50 jets a month.

eral Hodges' First Army. The two forces had done the job expected of them in just three weeks: Their massive drive had cut Germany into helpless halves separated by a wide corridor reaching from the Rhine to the Elbe. There was nothing left for them to do but to mop up their fronts, then sit tight and wait for the war to end. Henceforth, the burden of the April fighting lay to the north and the south.

On the northern front, the first three weeks of April were a frustrating time for Field Marshal Montgomery. To begin with, he had lost Berlin as his objective and also the use of the U.S. Ninth Army. The ultimate goals of the British Second Army were now to be the northern reaches of the Elbe River and Germany's ports on the North Sea. Montgomery fully appreciated the importance of capturing those ports speedily; he must deny them to the oncoming Russians in accordance with Churchill's determination to deny Stalin an outlet on the North Sea. But as Montgomery later declared, without the U.S. Ninth Army his various operations "would take longer than I had previously hoped."

In the northwest, where the front arched in the vicinity of the Dutch town of Nijmegen, Montgomery's Canadian First Army had to contend with a tricky problem that the Americans no longer faced. Northern Holland was still occupied by the Germans—about 120,000 of them under the capable General Blaskowitz; the Canadians would have to attack with restraint so as to avoid harming Britain's long-suffering Dutch allies.

At first, the campaign went briskly for the Canadians. After they had broken out of their bridgehead near Emmerich, some units drove northeast toward the North Sea, and the I Corps raced north toward the salty expanse of the Zuider Zee. But the northern attack ground to a halt on April 5 after covering barely 10 miles. Ahead lay the Neder River and Arnhem, the target of the Allies' ill-starred airborne assault in September 1944.

For one week, the Canadians made repeated feints at crossing the Neder River in front of Arnhem. Then, when the German forces were concentrated around that point, the British 49th Infantry Regiment, which was attached to the Canadian First Army, worked its way a few miles to the east, crossed the river there with little difficulty and then roared back westward to attack Arnhem from the rear on April 14.

Four days later, the Canadians reached the Zuider Zee—and an excruciating stalemate. They were eager to liberate the region immediately; its population had suffered a cruel famine all winter and was known to be on the verge of mass starvation. But if the Canadians attacked, the Germans might dynamite the dikes and flood hundreds of square miles. Montgomery was loath to risk the safety of the people he was trying to help. His forces stopped in place while Allied representatives negotiated with the Reich Commissioner of the Netherlands, Arthur Seyss-Inquart.

The Allied envoys proposed unconditional surrender or a temporary truce that would permit relief operations to the starving Dutch in the cities of the north. Seyss-Inquart turned down both alternatives, explaining that all Germans must fight until they received orders to the contrary from their government. Nevertheless, an informal truce took effect, and the German forces made no effort to close with the Canadians. After four days, British and American bombers began air-dropping food to the Dutch cities. Soon afterward, larger quantities of relief supplies began heading north by truck convoy.

In the meantime, Montgomery's British Second Army was pressing the offensive it had begun on March 28 when it broke out of its Wesel bridgehead on the Rhine. But the unit's progress was spotty. On the right flank beside the U.S. Ninth Army, the British VIII Corps moved ahead briskly, helped in large part by the Americans' devastating breakthrough in the center. Even though opposition was only light and sporadic, the VIII Corps was repeatedly held up while its engineers replaced bridges blown up by the Germans; they built 500 bridges in the course of their advance. The corps reached Minden by April 5 and Celle by April 10. But as the troops neared the area of Uelzen on April 14, they ran into resistance from the same energetic force that had been pestering the Americans to the south: General Wenck's Twelfth Army. The Germans, troops of Division Clausewitz, were ill-equipped and content with occasional hit-and-run attacks. All the same, they slowed down the VIII Corps. The British did not reach the Elbe until April 19.

To the north of the VIII Corps, the going was rough for the British XXX Corps, commanded by General Horrocks of Operation *Veritable* fame. Along the Dortmund-Ems Canal near Lingen, the troops ran into withering fire from the rem-

Using what cover they can find, Canadian First Army troops fight their way into the center of Arnhem, where fires set by the retreating Germans continue to burn. British paratroopers had failed miserably in their attempt to take the Dutch city during Operation Market-Garden in September 1944. But seven months later, on April 14, 1945, the Canadians mounted a powerful ground assault that liberated the city within 24 hours.

nants of General Student's First Parachute Army. On April 6 the British 3rd Division cleared the enemy out of Lingen, but German resistance grew stiffer as the XXX Corps pushed up the road toward the great port of Bremen. Wehrmacht and SS troops fiercely defended barricades at every crossroads, and as they retreated their engineers dynamited more bridges and several dams behind them. Not until April 19 did the British reach the outskirts of the city. The defenders of Bremen showed every intention of putting up a fight.

General Horrocks knew that his forces could take the city by storm. But the battle would be costly, not only to his own troops but to the port facilities as well. So on April 20 he offered Bremen a chance to surrender. Copies of his ultimatum were placed in 4,000 artillery shells specially designed to disseminate leaflets and were fired into the city. The ultimatum read: "The choice is yours. The British Army, supported by the RAF, is about to capture the city. There are two ways in which this can take place. Either by the employment of all the means at the disposal of the Army and RAF or by unconditional surrender. Yours is the responsibility for the unnecessary bloodshed that will result if you choose the first way. Otherwise you must send an envoy under the protection of a white flag over to the British lines."

The soldiers of the British Second Army settled down to wait for an answer. On the following day, the Germans commenced negotiations.

The southern front, where the two armies of General Devers' Sixth Army Group were on the attack, was a matter of nagging concern to General Eisenhower all through the first half of April. The French First Army, commanded by General Jean de Lattre de Tassigny, had been forced to leave a large part of its strength behind, west of the Rhine, to guard against any threat by German troops in northern Italy; as a result, the Frenchmen were having slow going in the steep hills and winding roads of the Black Forest region.

Since the French were so shorthanded, Patch's Seventh Army took on a disproportionate share of the Sixth Army Group's 120-mile front. Besides having to cover a wide front, the Seventh Army was running into strong opposition from the German First Army. Units of three divisions had to fight for 11 days before they could take the city of Heilbronn on the Neckar River.

To Eisenhower's great relief, Bradley's swift drive to the Elbe offered a chance to help Devers' armies. The U.S. First Army, firmly established on the Mulde by April 15 and with little more to do, could expand southward and take over some of the territory originally assigned to Patton's Third Army, freeing Patton for assignment farther south. At Ike's direction, Bradley ordered Patton to turn his army southeast into Austria for a linkup with the Russians near Salzburg. Patton's new course enabled his right-flank units to take over from Devers a strip of territory about 50 miles wide.

Eisenhower's realignment permitted Patch to send one of his corps, the VI, south into the Black Forest to help the French. This corps was to drive along the Neckar River past Stuttgart, then swing south to the Swiss border, trapping the German Nineteenth Army in the Black Forest. Meanwhile, the XV Corps, under General Wade Haislip, was veering southeast under earlier orders to take Bamberg and Nuremberg, which were being held by the German First Army under General Hermann Foertsch. Two of Haislip's divisions, the 3rd and the 45th, seized Bamberg with little trouble on April 13.

On the German side, Field Marshal Kesselring had realized in early April that an American drive toward Bamberg and Nuremberg was shaping up, and he had juggled his battered forces to counter it. The First Army—only 15,000 men but with 20 battalions of artillery—was already strung out on an 87-mile front extending from Heilbronn to Nuremberg, where it could cover the withdrawal of shattered German units into the mountains to the southeast. The remnants of two divisions, the 2nd Mountain and the 17th SS Panzer Grenadier, were ordered to rush to the aid of the Bamberg defenders. But a shortage of gasoline delayed them—and saved them for the defense of Nuremberg.

There the two divisions joined the 13th SS Corps under General Max Simon, who was preparing for a last-ditch defense. Simon was a tough and brutal SS officer whose troops had been responsible for a mass killing of Italian civilians when he was fighting partisans in 1944. In the week just past, Simon had held a drumhead trial of a number of war-weary German civilians, one of whom had attempted to disarm a contingent of Hitler Youth fighters. Simon had convicted and executed them all.

The stage was now set for the biggest single action of the April campaign in the west. Nuremberg would be defended to the bitter end, for ideological as well as strategic reasons. The walled and moated medieval city, ringed by bombed-out industrial and residential suburbs, had been lovingly described by Hitler as "the most German of all German cities." It was here in the prewar years that the immense and flamboyant Nazi Party rallies had been held. On these occasions as many as 500,000 of the party faithful jammed the massive Luitpold Arena on the city's outskirts while hand-picked divisions of the Wehrmacht and shovel-wielding battalions of the German Labor Front passed in review before their Führer.

The symbolic importance of defending the city had not been lost on local Nazi leaders. Gauleiter Karl Holz had promised Hitler that he would defend the city to the death. "I shall remain in this most German of all towns to fight and die," Holz had vowed. Hitler had responded by awarding Holz the Golden Cross of the German Order, one of the highest honors of the Third Reich.

General Haislip and his XV Corps, reinforced by the 42nd Division, closed in on Nuremberg on April 15, and by the next day they were in position to envelop the city. First, the 14th Armored Division had raced around to the southern and eastern approaches. There, at a distance of 15 miles from Nuremberg, the tanks had fanned out to block any counterattacks on the rear of the U.S. assault forces. Inside the armor's protective arc, the 45th Infantry Division had moved into jump-off positions in Nuremberg's southern and eastern suburbs. Meanwhile, the 3rd Infantry Division was poised to attack from the north, and the 42nd Infantry Division was moving into place in the western suburbs. On April 16 these forces began pushing toward the inner city, planning to squeeze the defenders into a tighter and tighter perimeter until they were crushed.

Inside the city, General Simon expected the main American thrust to come from the north and east. To meet it, he defended those sectors with his best units—the remnants of the 2nd Mountain and 17th SS Panzer Grenadier Divisions. The rest of his forces—home guardsmen, municipal police-

Generals Bradley (left), Patton and Eisenhower look through a cache of priceless paintings discovered by U.S. Third Army troops in a salt mine at Merkers in central Germany. The art treasures had been moved to Merkers from Berlin because, as the curator of the German state museums explained, "the Russians were pushing too close."

U.S. Third Army finance officers, assisted by a Reichsbank official, make an inventory of another treasure trove uncovered at Merkers: bags of money containing some 100 tons of gold bars and coins, plus three billion reichsmarks, and millions in American, British, French and Norwegian paper currency. This cache was discovered by an American MP when a German housewife pointed to the mine entrance and casually said, "That's where the bullion is hidden."

men and a mélange of survivors and stragglers—completed the defensive ring.

The advancing GIs soon discovered that Simon's forces packed a wallop out of all proportion to their numerical strength. The German commander had positioned hundreds of 88mm antiaircraft guns in a protective circle around the city, and the gunners fired their deadly 21-pound shells against the infantrymen of the 3rd and 45th Divisions. The projectiles, fused to burst overhead, scattered jagged metal fragments for hundreds of yards and left scores of infantrymen dead or writhing in agony.

The GIs also had to contend with another force, one that had become unfamiliar and whose sudden appearance underscored the importance that the Germans attached to Nuremberg: the Luftwaffe. On April 16, Messerschmitts and Focke-Wulf 190s flew 15 bombing and strafing sorties against the forward elements of the 45th Infantry Division. It was the heaviest air attack the division had encountered since invading German territory two months before. U.S. antiaircraft units engaged the enemy aircraft, sending three of them crashing in flames over the city.

To neutralize the Germans' 88mm guns, increasing numbers of tanks were soon poking precariously among Nuremberg's gigantic rubble piles and edging past enormous craters left by previous Allied air raids. One encounter between U.S. armor and the German 88s took place on the southern outskirts of the city when Sergeant Ben Bryan of the U.S. 106th Cavalry Group spotted nine of the big German guns. Bryan called up two tanks, which knocked out four of the guns with direct hits. Meanwhile, Bryan and his fellow cavalrymen picked off two gun crews with their carbines. At this, the three remaining gun crews waved white flags, and a dozen Germans came forward to surrender.

Sergeant Bryan exposed himself momentarily to gesture the 12 prisoners toward the rear. He was killed instantly by a blast from an 88mm shell, and the German prisoners took off, hoping to escape in the confusion.

Bryan's buddies realized that the Germans had duped them with an old trick: They had left one or two gunners in place while the others went forward to distract the Americans. Angered by their own naïveté as much as the Germans' duplicity, the cavalrymen opened fire with carbines and rifles, mowing down the 12 escaping prisoners. Then, advancing under cover of tanks, they killed the gunners.

It was only one example of the German desperation measures the GIs would encounter in the next four days of battle. The Germans booby-trapped the bodies of fallen comrades, knowing many GIs would search them for souvenirs. And they armed civilian volunteers with rifles and deadly *Panzerfaust* antitank weapons, whose shaped charges could penetrate eight inches of armor plating.

These civilians, some of them children in their teens, lurked at second-story windows with their *Panzerfausts* and took pot shots at passing tanks and personnel carriers. Other civilians hid in dugouts and basements until U.S. patrols had passed by and then popped out to shoot the GIs in the back. Against this type of opposition, the GIs became ruthless. If tankers saw *Panzerfaust* grenades coming from any

house, they swiveled their cannon and blasted the place into rubble. Foot patrols spared no grenades or submachine-gun bullets in flushing snipers from rubble piles and digging out enemy units from buildings room by room. This sort of bloody work went on all through April 16 and 17.

By the night of April 17, two thirds of the city was under American control. The 3rd Infantry Division had knocked out more than 50 heavy guns, while the 45th Infantry had smashed or captured 45 guns and taken almost 5,000 prisoners. But German resistance became even more furious as the Americans neared the inner walls of the ancient city.

Most GIs shunned risky heroics, and most of their officers did not call for attacks that might entail high casualties; it was too late in the War for that. "When the commanding generals of the 3rd and 45th Divisions impatiently telephone the regiments to get their tails busting and move forward faster," reported Time-Life correspondent Olson, "the colonels and the majors and the captains merely smile tolerantly and take their time."

Nevertheless, some GIs continued to fight with reckless bravery. On April 17 and 18, three infantrymen of the 3rd Division's 15th Regiment earned Medals of Honor for feats of arms far beyond the call of duty.

One of the three instances in particular is worth recording. Private Joseph F. Merrel's company was pinned down on April 18 in a hail of bullets from enemy rifles, machine pistols and two heavy machine guns. On his own initiative, Merrel made a 100-yard assault through enemy fire. Then, firing his rifle at almost point-blank range, he killed four Germans armed with machine pistols. As he started toward the nearest machine-gun emplacement, a bullet hit Merrel's rifle, leaving him armed with only three grenades.

Zigzagging to avoid increasing enemy fire, Merrel dashed another 200 yards and then heaved two grenades into the gun position. Before the smoke had cleared, he dived into the emplacement, grabbed a Luger pistol and dispatched the survivors of the grenade attack.

Rearmed, Merrel began crawling toward the second machine gun, 30 yards distant. En route he shot four more Germans in their foxholes. Then his luck ran out. A German bullet ripped into his body, wounding him critically in the abdomen. Bleeding profusely, Merrel managed to stagger on. Then, mustering his last reserves of strength, he heaved his remaining grenade at the machine gun and stumbled forward firing his Luger, wiping out survivors as he went.

All of a sudden, a burst of German fire caught Merrel squarely, killing him instantly. He had accounted for 23 enemy soldiers.

The Americans ground forward steadily. On the 18th, infantrymen of the 45th Division overran the huge Luitpold Arena. The GIs captured a group of SS troopers and Wehrmacht soldiers huddled under the stadium's concrete stands. At the sight of Americans on this hallowed Nazi ground, many of the German prisoners broke down and wept.

By April 19, the majority of Nuremberg's defenders had retreated into the inner city. General Simon, barricaded in his headquarters in an ancient citadel, dashed off impossible orders to the fragmented remnants of his forces—an SS unit here, a band of Hitler Youth there, even a force of 150

U.S. Seventh Army troops use submachine guns (right) and a light tank (far right) to break into a prisoner-of-war camp near Hammelburg, which they overran on April 6. The camp originally contained some 1,500 American prisoners, but only 75 sick and wounded GIs were on hand to cheer the liberators: In line with their policy of preventing the recapture of POWs, the Germans had evacuated the remainder in forced marches to camps that were still secure from the onrushing Americans.

city firemen pressed into service as infantrymen. Although most of the 88s had been destroyed or captured by now, these diehard units still poured out a continuous hail of bullets and *Panzerfaust* grenades on the tightening ring of American infantry and armor.

Bobbing and weaving through this fire, a regiment of the 3rd Division closed in on the inner city's north wall late on the evening of April 19. Advance patrols seized a gate in the wall and held it while other units of the division poured through. In the meantime, a regiment of the 45th Division blasted an opening through the south wall and advanced to meet the 3rd Division at the Pegnitz River, which coursed through the old city.

Realizing that the end was very near now, Gauleiter Karl Holz dispatched a final message to Hitler, including a greeting for the Führer's birthday on April 20: "My Führer! Nuremberg is surrounded on all sides. The enemy has fought his way into the inner city. He has suffered heavy casualties. Up to now 24 tanks have been put out of commission, 18 of them by *Panzerfaust*. All day long artillery and grenade fire falls into the burning city. Our casualties are also heavy. All antitank guns have been destroyed. There is an acute shortage of ammunition.

"The cooperation with the combat commander is excellent. All party members greet each other with 'Heil Hitler!' Our faith, our love, our life belongs to you, my Führer."

Holz then led a reckless counterattack against the 3rd Division regiment that had broken into the inner city in the north. Advancing steadily into withering American fire, Holz's force at one point threatened the forward line of an entire U.S. battalion. But after an hour of fighting, a determined stand by one company of GIs finally stopped the Germans. As dawn broke on April 20, Holz withdrew to an underground headquarters, having suffered heavier casualties than he had inflicted.

By now the increasing weight of U.S. artillery fire had driven all but the most fanatical Germans underground. Most sought shelter in a labyrinth of ancient tunnels that ran under the old city. The tunnels were already overcrowded with more than 10,000 homeless civilians who had been squatters there for months.

Living conditions were intolerable. Allied shelling had burst a water main, cutting off water supplies. Organized food distribution had stopped eight days earlier. On April 19 someone discovered an underground liquor warehouse, and after hundreds of people had slaked their thirst with wine and schnapps, rioting broke out.

There in the bowels of the old city, a German civilian who had seen too much war began a remarkable personal struggle to end the fighting. He was Andreas Mueller, the 54-year-old owner of a local automobile repair shop. Mueller decided that the only way to save his fellow civilians was to surrender the city. Taking matters into his own hands, Mueller demanded that a liaison officer send a radio message to General Simon requesting immediate surrender of the city. "Nuremberg," replied Simon from his citadel headquarters, "will be defended to the last bullet."

Mueller next turned to Nuremberg's Nazi mayor, Willi Liebel, who was with Gauleiter Holz in an underground command post in another sector of the city. Again Mueller's

186

request was rebuffed. "One more word," Liebel radioed, "and you will be executed."

Mueller was a man who believed in observing formalities. So he again radioed General Simon and informed him that he himself would negotiate the terms of surrender with the Americans. Enraged, Simon shot back, "I am sending a detachment immediately to arrest you." By then Mueller was already gone, searching for a tunnel he hoped would lead him beneath the fighting to the American positions.

Working his way through the underground maze, Mueller came upon a remote corridor. At the far end of this cold and dripping passageway, Mueller squeezed himself into a water-main tunnel barely large enough to accommodate a man alongside the pipes. On all fours, Mueller crawled through the tunnel for an hour and a half. At last, he pushed open an iron door, looked into a cellar and saw 10 surprised GIs staring back.

Mueller quickly explained his mission to the Americans, and a lieutenant volunteered to lead him to the American command post. There Mueller was given two surrender documents to present to German authorities. With these and a safe conduct pass, he returned to the American-held cellar and made his way back to the German lines.

Mueller began his search for someone in authority to sign the surrender documents. Gauleiter Holz and Mayor Liebel were his first candidates, even though they had threatened him. But by the morning of April 20, the American forces had occupied almost the entire old city and were rooting the remaining defenders out of cellars and tunnels. In an apparent suicide pact, Holz had shot Liebel and then turned his gun on himself. Another possibility was removed when General Simon was taken prisoner on the evening of April 20. American troops overran the citadel and captured the general along with 400 men.

But pockets of Germans were still holding out, and Mueller persisted in his mission. He finally found some officials to sign his surrender documents: Nuremberg's second and third deputy mayors. He led them to the U.S. command post, where they signed the capitulation terms. At last Andreas Mueller had completed his self-appointed task.

The five-day-long battle had taken a heavy toll of the defenders and the city itself. An estimated 1,500 Germans were dead or wounded, and 17,000 others had surrendered. The beautiful old city, already wrecked by Allied bombing before the attack began, was now completely in ruins. "On the day the old city fell," reported Time-Life correspondent Charles Wertenbaker, "there was nothing to be seen but mile after square mile of crumbled buildings, with here a wall or a tower standing and there a column of smoke rising. The fresh fires looked almost cheerful in the midst of so much desolation."

Word of the fall of Nuremberg was only a fraction of the bad news Hitler received on his 56th birthday. In the northwest, Montgomery's Canadians had turned east to clear the German coast between the Dutch border and the Weser River. On the Canadians' right, Montgomery's British units were about to move into Bremen and had driven to within 60 miles of the great fire-gutted port of Hamburg.

To the right of the British, Simpson's U.S. Ninth Army had cleared Magdeburg and tightened its grip on the Elbe from Wittenberge south to Barby. On Simpson's right, Hodges' First Army was spreading southward along the Elbe, and German forces had surrendered Leipzig to a lowly infantry captain of the 2nd Division. On Hodges' right, Patton's Third Army was on a line running south to Bayreuth. On Patton's right, Patch's Seventh Army was advancing southward between Bayreuth and the Neckar River near Stuttgart. On Patch's right, the French First Army was moving to attack Stuttgart.

Worst of all for the Germans, the Red Army had reached Oranienburg, just 18 miles to the north of Berlin, and—inexplicably and horrifyingly—the Western Allies showed no interest in capturing the city before the fierce and vengeful Russians did.

All this bad news seemed to have no effect on Hitler as he accepted birthday greetings from his staff in Berlin. The Führer seemed to be cheerful, even hopeful. There had been some talk of Hitler leaving Berlin for safe refuge in the Bavarian Alps later that day. But he made no effort to depart.

Colonel Nicolaus von Below, Hitler's Luftwaffe adjutant, soon learned that the Führer was going to stay. Hitler spoke to him and announced a new plan in the same excited and exciting voice that had outlined many a victorious campaign. The great impending battle for Berlin, said Hitler, presented the Reich with one last chance to snatch a victory from defeat.

In Adolf Hitler Square in Nuremberg, troops of the U.S. Seventh Army celebrate their capture of the Nazi stronghold on April 20, 1945, with a review. Then, leaving one division behind to mop up Nuremberg, the Seventh Army resumed its drive toward the city of Munich, which General Eisenhower described as "the cradle of the Nazi beast."

THE GIS AND THE GERMANS

Taking no chances, a leading citizen of the town of Blankenheim holds white flags in both fists as he approaches a group of U.S. Third Army soldiers.

SLIPPING INTO THE ROLE OF OCCUPIER

A woman puts a package of shotgun cartridges on a pile of weapons turned in by the people of Rubeland after its capture by the First Army.

Early in March 1945, a military policeman directing traffic at a crossroads in the Rhineland was collared by a frustrated U.S. Ninth Army colonel who demanded: "How damn far do I have to go to see this damn war?"

The kind of war the colonel expected was becoming harder to find. In some areas, German resistance seemed to dissolve. In one bomb-blasted city after another, GIs found exhausted citizens eager to renounce their past; the people of München Gladbach were busily painting over faded Nazi Party wall slogans when the Americans raced into town.

Almost to a man, the troops waved away the Germans' show of repentance. "These people seem to think," said Lieut. Colonel Tim Cook of the 83rd Division, "that if they take down their Nazi flags and scratch out Hitler's face on the big portrait on the wall of their front parlor, they're automatically anti-Nazis and our bosom buddies. I just don't trust any of these bastards."

Nevertheless, the Americans had to start shouldering the responsibilities of the conqueror. The collapsing German war machine was burdening the Americans with millions of displaced persons and prisoners of war, and the small military-government units originally assigned to feed and shelter these victims were soon overwhelmed.

Increasingly, units of combat troops were detailed to police captured towns and get them back on their feet. Shopkeepers' merchandise and citizens' belongings had to be protected from looters—German and American alike. U.S. soldiers found themselves attempting to reestablish municipal governments and to locate horses to help local farmers plant new crops.

Innumerable Americans were abruptly converted from fighting men to laborers. Artillerymen on bulldozers swept mounds of smoldering rubble from the streets. In ruined churches, infantrymen went to work sealing blown-out windows to prevent rain damage, and combat engineers dug underground to repair sheared electrical lines and broken water mains. There was an irksome irony to it all: The victors were now cleaning up for the vanquished.

A GI contemplates a symbol of German defeat—a pair of bronze lions that have been toppled from the victory arch on the Ludwigstrasse in Munich.

Reclining in the turret of his armored car, a Ninth Army soldier returns the curious attention of hundreds of civilians in the just-captured town of Jüchen.

SUBMISSIVE SMILES FOR THE GI CONQUERORS

As the GIs rolled into the German towns and cities, the victors and vanquished had a first tense look at each other. "It was all smiles, subservience and docility," observed a reporter who traveled with the Ninth Army through the Rhineland. "Most of the civilians seem determined to make friends with their conquerors."

As a matter of fact, the First Army's march into Cologne had the appearance of a homecoming celebration. The owners of the taverns that were still standing passed out wine and beer to the troops. Citizens who had suffered two dozen Allied air attacks lined the streets, calling out: "At last you have come! We have waited years for you!" The First Army brass pronounced the Germans' reception "terrific," but the GIs were skeptical.

In other towns—most often those with scant bomb damage—the air was chillier. The Wagnerian festival town of Bayreuth rallied its home guard for one last, utterly futile fight rather than surrendering meekly. The American troops obliged them, blasting the town with artillery fire.

With a white flag flying, a group of German townspeople peer anxiously from their makeshift shelter at approaching U.S. troops.

BÜRGERMEISTERS IN BATTLE JACKETS

In the course of their stay in a captured town, the troops of a combat unit worked with or in place of an American Military Government team to provide the town with a mayor, a police force and some all-round handymen.

The work was endless. Civilians were rounded up, registered and assigned to labor details. Occupation regulations were posted and enforced, among them a restriction on trips that would necessitate traveling more than three miles from town.

Any exemptions from the regulations required the signature of the American officer in charge. So did thousands of registration cards, requisition forms for supplies and other military paper work. One detachment commander, drafted as an AMG administrator, reported that he had scribbled his name 540,000 times within a one-month period.

The Americans also tackled a job of more lasting importance than the immediate emergencies and shortages they found in the town. They began questioning local citizens in a search for administrators—preferably anti-Nazis—who were capable enough to be put in charge of a new municipal government.

An American sound truck announces regulations to Germans assembled in a Cologne square. All-night curfews were enforced until the fighting had moved o

Led by a GI, citizens of Erkelenz file toward a registration point. Some people, fearful of looters, carry bundles of prized possessions.

An antitank ditch blocking one of the major thoroughfares in Düsseldorf is filled by a labor detail of local men, women and children.

Piles of crated records and unused clothing are tended by a soldier inside a church in the Bavarian town of Ellingen. The church had been used by the Naz

Using candles because the power is still out, a GI and Cologne officials read Nazi records in a bank vault.

s a secret depot for clothing requisitioned from France and the Netherlands.

Beethoven's birthplace in Bonn is made off limits to dissuade looters.

A Ninth Army soldier proudly shows off his collection of German souvenirs, including a bayonet, a pair of pistols and a Nazi sword.

THE SPOILS AND PLEASURES OF VICTORY

At every opportunity, the Americans in Germany exercised the prerogatives of the winner. Occupied towns were a scavenger's—or a thief's—delight. GIs combed the piles of surrendered German weapons for coveted souvenirs—particularly Walther automatic pistols and fancy SS daggers. Some men, in violation of a loosely enforced regulation, ransacked the homes in which they were billeted. In Berneck an observer saw a company of engineers carting away "odd pieces of bedding and furniture, stoves, cooking utensils and a host of other paraphernalia that made their convoys look like gypsy caravans."

Some of the GIs specialized in improving their diets. Chickens, eggs and potatoes were confiscated from nearby farms. Rivers and ponds were fished the easy way—with hand grenades. And many a late-night poker game or songfest was enlivened by bottles of good Rhine wine "liberated" from someone's cellar.

Seventh Army troops take the view from atop a 274mm railroad gun. Countless cannon and vehicles were abandoned by fleeing Germans.

GIs tap kegs of beer they found in a Rhineland stronghold. In the foreground are two Panzerfausts—antitank grenade launchers.

A warning sign, posted by an American vanguard near a river crossing, tells a familiar story to the advancing motorized infantry.

Men of the 2nd Armored Division quit a German village to press across the Weser River early in April. That night, the tankers fought off stubborn fire from enemy field guns, mortars and small arms. The war was not yet won.

BIBLIOGRAPHY

Baldwin, Hanson W., "Our 'Rubber Cows.'" *The New York Times Magazine*, February 1, 1942.

Battle Babies: The Story of the 99th Infantry Division in World War II. Military Press of Louisiana, 1951.

Binkoski, Joseph, and Arthur Plaut, *The 115th Infantry Regiment in World War II*. Infantry Journal Press, 1948.

Blumenson, Martin, *The Patton Papers 1940-1945*. Houghton Mifflin, 1957.

Boice, William S., ed., *History of the Twenty-Second United States Infantry in World War II*. Dr. William S. Boice, 1959.

Bowman, Waldo G., *American Military Engineering in Europe: From Normandy to the Rhine*. Engineering News-Record, no date.

Bradley, Omar N., *A Soldier's Story*. Henry Holt, 1951.

Brett-Smith, Richard, *Hitler's Generals*. Presidio Press, 1976.

Briggs, Richard A., *The Battle of the Ruhr Pocket*. Tioga Book Press, 1957.

Bryant, Arthur, *Triumph in the West*. Doubleday, 1959.

Burck, Gilbert, "Ruhr, Second Battle of Germany." *Fortune*, December 1946.

Canadian Army:
War Diary of 1st Bn, The Royal Winnipeg Rifles. 1945.
War Diary of Headquarters 8th Canadian Infantry Brigade. 1945.
War Diary of Headquarters 7th Canadian Infantry Brigade. 1945.

Capa, Robert, *Slightly Out of Focus*. Henry Holt, 1947.

Cheves, Wallace R., ed., *Snow Ridges & Pillboxes: A True History of the 274th Infantry Regiment of the 70th Division in World War II*. Third Army, no date.

Colbaugh, Jack, *The Bloody Patch: A True Story of the Daring 28th Infantry Division*. Vantage Press, 1973.

Cole, Hugh M., *United States Army in World War II, The European Theater of Operations, The Ardennes: Battle of the Bulge*. Office of the Chief of Military History, U.S. Army, 1965.

Coll, Blanche D., Jean E. Keith, and Herbert H. Rosenthal, *United States Army in World War II, The Technical Services, The Corps of Engineers: Troops and Equipment*. Office of the Chief of Military History, U.S. Army, 1958.

Combat History of the Second Infantry Division in World War II. Second Infantry Division Headquarters, 1946.

Conquer: The Story of Ninth Army 1944-1945. Infantry Journal Press, 1947.

Cooper, Matthew, *The German Army 1933-1945*. Macdonald and Jane's, 1978.

Craven, Wesley Frank, and James Lea Cate, eds., *The Army Air Forces in World War II*, Vol. 3, *Europe: Argument to V-E Day (January 1944 to May 1945)*. University of Chicago Press, 1951.

Dachau. U.S. Seventh Army, 1945.

De Guingand, Sir Francis, *Operation Victory*. Hodder and Stoughton, 1947.

De Lattre de Tassigny, Jean, *The History of the French First Army*. Transl. by Malcolm Barnes. George Allen and Unwin, 1952.

Deveikis, Casey, *The Eager Beaver Regiment: The Regimental History of the 1303 Engineers*. Casey Deveikis, 1952.

Devlin, Gerard M., *Paratrooper!* St. Martin's Press, 1979.

Donnison, F. S. V., *Civil Affairs and Military Government North-West Europe 1944-1946*. London: Her Majesty's Stationery Office, 1961.

Draper, Theodore, *The 84th Infantry Division in the Battle of Germany (November 1944—May 1945)*. Viking Press, 1946.

Eisenhower, Dwight D., *Crusade in Europe*. Doubleday, 1948.

Ellis, L. F., and A. E. Warhurst, *Victory in the West*, Vol. 2, *The Defeat of Germany*. London: Her Majesty's Stationery Office, 1968.

Elstob, Peter, *Battle of the Reichswald*. Ballantine Books, 1970.

Engineer Operations by the VII Corps in the European Theater, Vol. 1. U.S. Army, 1948.

Esposito, Vincent J., ed.:
A Concise History of World War II. Frederick A. Praeger, 1964.
The West Point Atlas of American Wars, Vol. 2, *1900-1953*. Frederick A. Praeger, 1959.

Essame, H., *The Battle for Germany*. Bonanza Books, 1969.

Ewing, Joseph H., *29 Let's Go!: A History of the 29th Infantry Division in World War II*. Infantry Journal Press, 1948.

Forced Crossing of the Rhine, 1945. U.S. Army Corps of Engineers, 1945.

Forty, George, *Patton's Third Army at War*. Charles Scribner's Sons, 1978.

Frankel, Nat, and Larry Smith, *Patton's Best: An Informal History of the 4th Armored Division*. Hawthorn Books, 1978.

Friedheim, Eric, "Rhineland Rendezvous." *Air Force Magazine*, May 1945.

Gavin, James M., *On to Berlin: Battles of an Airborne Commander 1943-1946*. Viking Press, 1978.

Giles, Janice Holt, ed., *The G.I. Journal of Sergeant Giles*. Houghton Mifflin, 1965.

Harr, Bill, *Combat Boots*. Exposition Press, 1952.

Heaps, Leo, *The Evaders*. William Morrow, 1976.

Hechler, Ken, *The Bridge at Remagen*. Ballantine Books, 1957.

Hewitt, Robert L., *Work Horse of the Western Front: The Story of the 30th Infantry Division*. Infantry Journal Press, 1946.

A History of the Black Cats from Texas to France, Germany and Austria and Back to California. U.S. Army Thirteenth Armored Division, 1945.

Hoegh, Leo A., and Howard J. Doyle, *Timberwolf Tracks: The History of the 104th Infantry Division 1942-1945*. Infantry Journal Press, 1946.

Houston, Donald E., *Hell on Wheels: The 2d Armored Division*. Presidio Press, 1977.

Humble, Richard, *Hitler's Generals*. Doubleday, 1974.

Huston, James A., *Out of the Blue*. Purdue University Studies, 1972.

Icks, Robert J., *Tanks and Armored Vehicles 1900-1945*. WE Inc., no date.

Kesselring, Albert, *Kesselring: A Soldier's Record*. William Morrow, 1954.

Maass, Walter B., *The Netherlands at War: 1940-1945*. Abelard-Schuman, 1970.

MacDonald, Charles B.:
Airborne. Ballantine Books, 1970.
The Mighty Endeavor. Oxford University Press, 1969.
United States Army in World War II, The European Theater of Operations, The Last Offensive. Office of the Chief of Military History, U.S. Army, 1973.
United States Army in World War II, The European Theater of Operations, The Siegfried Line Campaign. Office of the Chief of Military History, U.S. Army, 1963.

McKee, Alexander, *The Race for the Rhine Bridges: 1940, 1944, 1945*. Stein and Day, 1971.

Macksey, K. J., *Panzer Division: The Mailed Fist*. Ballantine Books, 1968.

Manchester, William, *The Arms of Krupp 1587-1968*. Bantam Books, 1968.

Mellenthin, F. W. von, *German Generals of World War II As I Saw Them*. University of Oklahoma Press, 1977.

Mick, Allan H., ed., *With the 102d Infantry Division through Germany*. Infantry Journal Press, no date.

Montgomery, Bernard Law, *The Memoirs of Field-Marshal the Viscount Montgomery of Alamein, K.G.* World Publishing, 1958.

Morison, Samuel Eliot, *History of United States Naval Operations in World War II*, Vol. 11, *The Invasion of France and Germany 1944-1945*. Little, Brown, 1975.

Murphy, Audie, *To Hell and Back*. Bantam Books, 1949.

Patton, George S., Jr., *War As I Knew It*. Houghton Mifflin, 1947.

Pay, D. R., *Thunder from Heaven: Story of the 17th Airborne Division 1943-1945*. BOOTS, The Airborne Quarterly, 1947.

Persico, Joseph E., *Piercing the Reich*. Viking Press, 1979.

Pia, Jack, *Nazi Regalia*. Ballantine Books, 1971.

Pogue, Forrest C., *United States Army in World War II, The European Theater of Operations, The Supreme Command*. Office of the Chief of Military History, U.S. Army, 1954.

Powley, A. E., *Broadcast from the Front*. Toronto: A. M. Hakkert, 1975.

Reed, Arthur, and Roland Beaumont, *Typhoon and Tempest at War*. London: Ian Allan, 1974.

Richards, Denis, *Royal Air Force 1939-1945*, Vol. 1, *The Fight at Odds*. London: Her Majesty's Stationery Office, 1974.

Ruppenthal, Roland G., *United States Army in World War II, The European Theater of Operations, Logistical Support of the Armies*, Vol. 2, *September 1944—May 1945*. Office of the Chief of Military History, U.S. Army, 1959.

Rust, Kenn C., *The 9th Air Force in World War II*. Aero Publishers, 1967.

Ryan, Cornelius, *The Last Battle*. Popular Library, 1966.

Saunders, Hilary St. George, *Royal Air Force 1939-1945*, Vol. 3, *The Fight Is Won*. London: Her Majesty's Stationery Office, 1975.

Semmler, Rudolf, *Goebbels—The Man Next to Hitler*. London: Westhouse, 1947.

The Seventh United States Army in France and Germany 1944-1945, Vol. 3. Seventh United States Army, 1946.

78th Infantry Division Historical Association, eds., *Lightning: The History of the 78th Infantry Division*. Infantry Journal Press, 1947.

Shirer, William L., *The Rise and Fall of the Third Reich*. Simon and Schuster, 1960.

Simonds, Peter, *Maple Leaf Up, Maple Leaf Down: The Story of the Canadians in the Second World War*. Island Press, 1946.

Smith, Frank, *Battle Diary: The Story of the 243rd Field Artillery Battalion in Combat*. Hobson Book Press, 1946.

Smith, Marcus J., *The Harrowing of Hell: Dachau*. University of New Mexico Press, 1972.

Smith, Walter Bedell, *Eisenhower's Six Great Decisions (Europe 1944-1945)*. Longmans, Green, 1956.

Snyder, Louis C., *Encyclopedia of the Third Reich*. McGraw-Hill, 1976.

Spearhead in the West. U.S. Army, 3rd Armored Division, 1945.

Speer, Albert, *Inside the Third Reich*. Macmillan, 1970.

Stacey, Charles P., *Official History of the Canadian Army in the Second World War*, Vol. 3, *The Victory Campaign: The Operations in North-West Europe 1944-1945*. Ottawa: The Queen's Printer and Controller of Stationery, 1960.

Stamps, T. Dodson, and Vincent J. Esposito, eds., *A Military History of World War II*, Vol. 1, *Operations in the European Theaters*. United States Military Academy, 1953.

Thompson, R. W., *The Battle for the Rhineland*. London: Hutchinson & Co., 1958.

Timothy, P. H., *The Rhine Crossing: Twelfth Army Group Engineer Operations*. Chief Engineer, Twelfth Army Group, no date.

Toland, John, *The Last 100 Days*. Random House, 1965.

Van der Zee, Henri A., *The Hunger Winter: Occupied Holland 1944-45*. London: Macmillan, publication forthcoming.

Whiting, Charles:
Battle of the Ruhr Pocket. Ballantine Books, 1970.
Bradley. Ballantine Books, 1971.

Wilmot, Chester, *The Struggle for Europe*. Harper & Row, 1952.

Ziemke, Earl F., *The U.S. Army in the Occupation of Germany, 1944-1946*. Center of Military History, U.S. Army, 1975.

Zink, Harold, *American Military Government in Germany*. Macmillan, 1947.

PICTURE CREDITS

Credits from left to right are separated by semicolons, from top to bottom by dashes.

COVER and page 1: U.S. Army.

BUILD-UP FOR A NEW D-DAY—6, 7: William Vandivert for *Life*. 8: National Archives. 9: U.S. Army. 10, 11: U.S. Navy, National Archives. 12, 13: U.S. Army; National Archives. 14, 15: William Vandivert for *Life* (3); National Archives; William Vandivert for *Life*—U.S. Army—William Vandivert for *Life*. 16, 17: Tallandier, Paris.

INVADING THE THIRD REICH—20, 21: Map by Tarijy Elsab. 22: Imperial War Museum, London. 23: U.S. Army. 25: Ullstein Bilderdienst, Berlin (West). 26, 27: George Silk for *Life*. 28: National Archives. 29: Map by Tarijy Elsab. 30: U.S. Army. 32: The Public Archives of Canada/D.N.D., Ottawa (C-46504); ADN-Zentralbild, Berlin, DDR. 34: U.S. Army.

THE ORDEAL ON THE ROER—36, 37: U.S. Army. 38: William Vandivert for *Life*. 39: U.S. Army. 40-43: George Silk for *Life*. 44, 45: Johnny Florea for *Life*; U.S. Army.

THE RACE FOR THE BRIDGES—48: U.S. Army. 49: Map by Tarijy Elsab. 51: National Archives. 53: U.S. Army. 54: Associated Press, London. 55: Margaret Bourke-White for *Life*. 56: Wide World. 57: U.S. Army; United Press International. 58: U.S. Army.

HOLLAND'S "HUNGER WINTER"—60, 61: Rijksinstituut voor Oorlogsdocumentatie, Amsterdam. 62: Charles Breyer, Hilversum. 63: M. C. Meyboom, courtesy Cas Oorthuys Archives, Amsterdam. 64: Cas Oorthuys Archives, Amsterdam. 65: Charles Breyer, Hilversum. 66: Kryn Taconis, courtesy Cas Oorthuys Archives, Amsterdam. 67: J. Van Rhijn, Rotterdam. 68, 69: The Prentenkabinet of Leyden University, Leyden (2); Emmy Andriesse, courtesy Cas Oorthuys Archives, Amsterdam—Emmy Andriesse, courtesy The Prentenkabinet of Leyden University, Leyden; Cas Oorthuys Archives, Amsterdam—Emmy Andriesse, courtesy The Prentenkabinet of Leyden University, Leyden. 70: The Public Archives of Canada/D.N.D., Ottawa (C-50424). 71: Kryn Taconis, Toronto.

"THE ENEMY CANNOT ESCAPE"—75: Map by Tarijy Elsab. 76: Bundesarchiv, Koblenz. 78: U.S. Army. 80, 81: E.C.P. Armées, Paris, except top right, Wide World. 84: George Rodger for *Life*. 86, 87: Imperial War Museum, London—U.S. Air Force; Imperial War Museum, London; U.S. Air Force. 90, 91: U.S. Army, except top left, National Archives.

A LAST GREAT AIRDROP—94-96: Robert Capa from Magnum for *Life*. 97: Robert Capa from Wide World. 98-113: Robert Capa from Magnum for *Life*.

HURDLING THE FINAL BARRIER—114, 115: George Rodger for *Life*. 116: United Press International. 117: U.S. Army. 118, 119: U.S. Army, except bottom left, National Archives. 120, 121: Wide World; William Vandivert for *Life*. 122, 123: William Vandivert for *Life*, except bottom right, U.S. Army. 124, 125: Keystone Press Agency Ltd., London; U.S. Army.

ASSAULT ON "FORTRESS RUHR"—128: Map by Tarijy Elsab. 130: U.S. Army. 131: Zalewski/Rapho, Paris—U.S. Army (2); Imperial War Museum, London (2). 133: Wide World. 134-137: U.S. Army. 138: Johnny Florea for *Life*. 139-141: U.S. Army.

THE RAMPAGING AMERICANS—144, 145: U.S. Army. 146: William Vandivert for *Life*. 147: George Silk for *Life*. 148, 149: U.S. Army, except top left, Imperial War Museum, London. 150, 151: U.S. Army. 152, 153: U.S. Army, except top left, Wide World. 154, 155: U.S. Army, except top left, William Vandivert for *Life*. 156, 157: U.S. Army.

FREEING THE CAMPS OF DEATH—158, 159: Wide World. 160: Margaret Bourke-White for *Life*. 161: Imperial War Museum, London. 162, 163: George Rodger for *Life*—David E. Scherman for *Life*; Wide World. 164, 165: U.S. Army; Margaret Bourke-White for *Life*. 166, 167: National Archives; George Rodger for *Life*—Wide World. 168, 169: Bildarchiv Preussischer Kulturbesitz, Berlin (West)—U.S. Army; Wide World.

PURSUIT TO THE ELBE—173: Associated Press, London. 174, 175: Robert Capa from Magnum for *Life*. 176: U.S. Army. 178: U.S. Air Force. 179: Wide World. 181: United Press International. 182: U.S. Army. 183: Wide World. 184: United Press International. 185: U.S. Army. 186: Wide World.

THE GIS AND THE GERMANS—188-190: U.S. Army. 191: United Press International. 192, 193: U.S. Army; Wide World. 194, 195: Margaret Bourke-White for *Life*; U.S. Army (2). 196, 197: U.S. Army; Margaret Bourke-White for *Life*—Bundesarchiv, Koblenz. 198, 199: William Vandivert for *Life*—United Press International; U.S. Army. 200, 201: Johnny Florea for *Life*; William Vandivert for *Life*.

ACKNOWLEDGMENTS

For help given in the preparation of this book, the editors wish to express their gratitude to Association Rhin-Danube, Paris; Alfred M. Beck, U.S. Army Corps of Engineers, Office of the Chief of Engineers, Washington, D.C.; Hans Becker, ADN-Zentralbild, Berlin, DDR; Carole Boutté, Senior Researcher, U.S. Army Audio-Visual Activity, The Pentagon, Arlington, Virginia; Phyllis S. Cassler, U.S. Army Military History Institute, Carlisle Barracks, Pennsylvania; Huguette Chalufour, Éditions Jules Tallandier, Paris; V. M. Destefano, Chief of Research Library, U.S. Army Audio-Visual Activity, The Pentagon, Arlington, Virginia; Dr. Joyce Eakin, U.S. Army Military History Institute, Carlisle Barracks, Pennsylvania; Dr. Matthias Haupt, Bundesarchiv, Koblenz, Germany; Werner Haupt, Bibliothek für Zeitgeschichte, Stuttgart, Germany; Dr. Carl H. Hermann, Rheinbach, Germany; Robert C. Hurley, Lutherville, Maryland; Dr. Robert Klein, McGraw-Hill Publications Company, Chicago, Illinois; Dr. Roland Klemig, Bildarchiv Preussischer Kulturbesitz, Berlin (West); Samuel E. Klippa, Pittsburgh, Pennsylvania; Madame La Maréchale de Lattre de Tassigny, Paris; William H. Leary, National Archives and Records Service, Audio-Visual Division, Washington, D.C.; Marianne Loenartz, Bundesarchiv, Koblenz, Germany; Thomas D. Lucey, Frankfurt-am-Main, Germany; Colonel William D. Lynch, USA (Ret.), Washington, D.C.; Charles B. MacDonald, Office of the Chief of Military History, U.S. Army Center of Military History, Washington, D.C.; Hendon A. R. Mack, Royal Air Force Museum, London; Walter Maxeiner, Saarlouis, Germany; Mr. Leonard Montone, Southern Music Publishing Co. Inc., New York, New York; Meinhard Nilges, Bundesarchiv, Koblenz, Germany; Mrs. Lydia Oorthuys-Krienen, Amsterdam; Yves Perret-Gentil, Comité d'Histoire de la Deuxième Guerre Mondiale, Paris; Janusz Piekalkiewicz, Rösrath-Hoffnungsthal, Germany; Brigadier General Jack T. Pink, USA (Ret.), Annandale, Virginia; Michel Rauzier, Comité d'Histoire de la Deuxième Guerre Mondiale, Paris; Major General Walter B. Richardson, USA (Ret.), New Braunfels, Texas; Reverend Franz Rötter, Ellingen, Germany; Rudolf Schub, Ellingen, Germany; Axel Schulz, Ullstein Bilderdienst, Berlin (West); R. Simpson, Royal Air Force Museum, London; Freiherr Colonel Hasso von Uslar-Gleichen, Embassy of the Federal Republic of Germany, Washington, D.C.; Henri A. van der Zee, London; Fran Weaver, Researcher, U.S. Army Audio-Visual Activity, The Pentagon, Arlington, Virginia; Carol Weinles, Post Librarian, Fort Myer, Virginia; Paul White, National Archives and Records Service, Audio-Visual Division, Washington, D.C.; Hannah Zeidlik, Office of the Chief of Military History, U.S. Army Center of Military History, Washington, D.C.

Lyrics to "Der Fuehrer's Face" copyright 1942 by Southern Music Publishing Co. Inc., copyright renewed, used by permission, all rights reserved.

The index for this book was prepared by Nicholas J. Anthony.

INDEX